Lean Six Sigma Guidebook

By Dennis Fisher
Daniel Farb
Bruce Gordon

By Daniel Farb and Bruce Gordon …

<u>Total Quality in Provider Practices</u> received five stars from ForewordReviews.com: "Excellent tool to assist any health care organization." It is available as a book, CD, or web course at www.uohc.com. It has many sections of interest to other industries, such as the easy to understand section on total quality statistics.

Please send any correspondence regarding permissions to:
UniversityOfHealthCare
419 N. Larchmont Blvd., #323
Los Angeles, CA 90004

Lean Six Sigma Guidebook

ISBN 13: 9781594912443
ISBN 10: 1594912440

Library of Congress Catalog Number: In process

UniversityOfHealthCare/ UniversityOfBusiness website:
www.uohc.com

Contents of Lean Six Sigma Guidebook

Authors

DENNIS FISHER, MBA, CFPIM, CPM is President of Basic Business Services, an international organization dedicated to education and consulting in the global business community. His business and personal life is founded on one key principle - To train and develop people for their personal and professional growth. Thus he is focused on the physical application of learning through the students. He has held many positions over the last 30 years in manufacturing, distribution, purchasing, consulting, training, engineering and service organizations.

Mr. Fisher is considered an industry leader in "Who's Who in Industry and Finance" and other reference publications for his contributions to automation and advanced process redesign throughout the world. He is a regular speaker at professional and civic groups around the world. He has served in the presidencies of several professional societies including the Institute for Supply Management and the American Production and Inventory Control Society.

Mr. Fisher received his MBA from Pepperdine University with a focus on Customer Satisfaction and Quality. He has undergraduate degrees in both Sociology and American Studies. In addition to his formal schooling, he also has earned professional certificates in Nuclear Technology, Paint Technology, Communications Electronics, Production Planning and Control, Purchasing Management and Professional Training.

Mr. Fisher has served as an Assistant Professor in several universities and colleges. He presents lectures, seminars, workshops, educational and certification programs in the US and in countries such as China, Japan, New Zealand, Europe, Caribbean, Mexico, Central America, and Canada. He has been a faculty member at Canadian Management Centre in Toronto, Canada for over 10 years.

Mr. Fisher has written and published many articles, essays, and books. He has been published in many domestic and international books, conference proceedings, and professional journals, including McGraw Hills' Production and Inventory Control Handbook, Auerback Publishers' Computers in Manufacturing, and McGraw Hills' The Just-In-Time Self Test and Implementation Guide.

M. DANIEL FARB, M.D., CEO of UniversityOfHealthCare and UniversityOfBusiness, is a leader in the field of interactive management and healthcare e-learning. He received a BA in English Literature from Yale (where he set an academic record and studied with writers like Robert Penn Warren), an M.D. from Boston University, a degree in Executive Management from the Anderson School of Business at UCLA, and is currently working on a degree at UCLA in International Trade. He is a practicing ophthalmologist. He also has received two patents in ophthalmology and is working on others in other fields, has worked with the World Health Organization in Geneva and the National Institutes of Health in Washington, D.C. He has written scientific and popular articles, and has worked as a newspaper reporter. He helped Dr. Robbins edit one of the editions of Robbins' "Pathology" textbook for readability. He wrote an article on humor for the Massachusetts Review. He has experience in theater and television, including acting, directing, and stage-managing. He has programmed his own patient records database. He has written and edited hundreds of e-learning courses, CDs, and books.

Dr. Farb is a member of the American Academy of Ophthalmology, the Union of American Physicians and Dentists, the AOJS, the American Association of Physicians and Surgeons, the American Society for Training and Development (ASTD), the E-Learning Forum, the Southern California Biomedical Council, the PDA (Parenteral Drug Association), and the Medical Marketing Association.

BRUCE GORDON is the Creative Director for UniversityOfHealthCare. After receiving a BA in Economics from UCLA, he began a freelance writing career that included technical writing (such as a manual for Princess Cruise Lines), stand-up comedy routines for nationally known comedians, and screenplay writing. He has done production support work with famous Hollywood personalities on such well-known productions as Aaron Spelling's "Dynasty" and "Love Boat" TV shows. An audio-visual software specialist, he is a versatile artist, with published works in a variety of media, including music, motion graphics, and digital video short film.

Introduction

This is a course in the form of a book. When you have completed it, you will have a great practical training on lean six sigma ("lean") operations.

This course teaches a process of maximizing the flow of business. The material is structured in two segments. The first segment explains the mechanisms of lean and the applications of lean mechanisms, that is, how they can be used. The second segment expands lean operations into support functions of business.

Course Outcomes

At the end of this course, you will be able to:

- Define what truly adds value to your business
- Discover how to seek out and eliminate waste from any and all processes
- Make flow charts that will highlight the waste within the flow of work
- Structure operational layouts that increase speed throughout the company
- Run and evaluate a Just-In-Time pull system
- Define and implement a lean measure board based on simplicity and improvement

The goal of lean operations is to improve the work areas by building a cellular process base. "Cellular manufacturing" means a manufacturing process that produces families of parts within a single line or cell of machines operated by machinists who work only within the line or cell. However, lean operations are not just for production. It also applies to offices, distribution, and other work systems.

Lean operations (abbreviated henceforth as simply "lean"), focuses on the following question each organization should ask of its operations: "What waste do we have in our systems?" Waste is any activity, materials, or capacity performed in any company activity that does not add value to the product or service. Human examples of the lean principle can be seen in the world of Olympic swimming and track. These gold medal-winning athletes typically have very minimal body fat, and they perform with no waste of motion or body system resources.

This course is a valuable asset for any company or organization wishing to achieve this same ideal. Just as with athletes, you will gain an advantage over your competitors by becoming very lean—that is, with no waste, no excess, no squandered time, and no loss of resources in any of the operational processes.

SEGMENT I:

Lean Mechanisms and Applications

Chapter 1: Going Lean - What Does it Mean?

Learning Objectives

- Define what truly adds value
- List what the customers want but seldom get
- Define the competitive advantages driven by lean thinking

In order to be a world-class operation, an organization must become lean. To achieve this, the organization must examine itself and determine the optimal way to perform its operations. This means getting rid of the organization's operational fat and waste. Areas to eliminate include unnecessary process time, disorganization, unnecessary handling, unneeded space, and all rework or redoing of any process. In fact, any word that begins with "re," such as redo, rework, rerun, recall, or reissue, usually indicates a prime target for "leaning" the process.

This examination should be the barometer in deciding how to improve the organization's processes. Unfortunately, many managers who seek improvement are only spinning their wheels, because their focus is simply on sections of what might add value. Only partially helpful in their own microcosms, they don't add overall value to the entire organization. The best improvements are achieved via an integrated approach that makes customer satisfaction the determining measured factor of choice. In this way, the benefits of the improvement campaign can be collected and returned to the process.

There are seven competitive advantages that a company can use to surpass another company in its business. The most common three are (1) quality, (2) price, and (3) delivery. Most people who purchase anything want the best quality and, of course, the best price. They also typically want on-time delivery. Purchasers also force companies to compete in the areas of (4) product design, which means quality of product, as well as (5) service and (6) image. (7) Flexibility is the final of the seven competitive advantages. The organization that can improve on each of these seven competitive advantages will win business from others who may not be striving to improve their appeal to customers in these fundamental and critical areas.

What Does Lean Mean?

- Speed to customers through manufacturing
- Waste minimized in the use of resources
- Time as the foremost resource

Also known as "Just In Time" (JIT), lean is a philosophy for operating organizations with planned elimination of all wasted resources and continuous improvement of productivity. The two basic rules of this mindset are to have *only* the required minimum amount of top quality inventory in the proper place at the exact time when needed. This involves all activities in all departments necessary to maintain the flow of materials through the company. The implication is that each operation is so closely synchronized with the subsequent ones, that the signal to perform work in any station comes from the downstream station. So no work is initiated in any station until the station downstream is ready for it. This eliminates the need for the processes of works in progress to wait between the stations. It also cuts out the need to stock the materials from those works in progress waiting between the stations.

Delivery and service time, as defined by the customer, have become paramount now. This is in contrast to the past, when money and manpower were considered to be the greatest resources.
For example, the reason most people have an ATM card is that they don't want to wait for the bank to be open to obtain services. Another example is credit card-enabled, self-serve gas stations, where the customer can get gasoline without seeing a station employee. This is because people don't have time to go to a cashier's window to pay for gas, and then come back out to pump it. Desiring to waste the least amount of time in obtaining the products and services they want, customers demand faster service.

Here is an example of acceleration in the movement of new products. Fifteen years ago, it took about 40-45 months to bring a car from original concept to production line. Within the last decade, the time spent to bring one to production decreased to about 12 months or even less. This means that now you could have a new product design every year. People just want that product or service – whatever you offer—much faster. Furthermore, they want the same quality and better pricing than they had before.

Lean also means optimized use of resources while giving maximized customer satisfaction.

Lean vs. Efficiency

The philosophy of lean is superior to the concept of efficiency. This is because lean is based upon an organization's actual productivity or through-put, meaning time and a person's output per time. Efficiency, however, is a suboptimal measure that just indicates how much work was completed as compared to a standard. But this standard is a static number, which means that the measure of efficiency can make an organization look good without adding any value. The main standard should be time spent, which should be constantly declining. Lean focuses on added value and not static standards; hence it is a much better philosophy.

Statements of Lean

- "I feel the need for speed!" (Quote from the movie "Top Gun")
- "If it stops, it costs!"
- "Doing more and more with less and less"
- "Value added vs. value wasted"
- "A journey, not a destination"
- "The continuous elimination of bottlenecks"

As stated above, speed is the most important asset that a company can have today. If a customer can place an order today and get it today—as opposed to next week—that creates a competitive advantage. If a company could respond quickly in solving problems or sending out products or services, then it would be more competitive than anybody else. In lean, a bottleneck means a facility, function, or department, etc., that impedes production—for example, a machine or work center, where jobs arrive at a faster rate than they can be completed.

Lean Manufacturing

- Specify the value of a product
- Identify the value stream of a product
- Make these values flow without interruption
- Pull the values to the customers
- Pursue perfection

The value of a product is first that it is in demand, that is, that people want it. It goes without saying that it must work properly. The value increases as you are able to provide it quickly, in the best format possible. Other things that can add value are delivering it with the right color, in the best kind of container, and with the best customer service. This means that you must understand the actual flow of a product from the company or organization that provides it to the customer that uses it, back to the company, and even back to the suppliers for the company's product.

Example: Consumer products as cosmetics, which have strict FDA regulations regarding chemical ingredients. Incorrect materials will result in a product that can't be sold.

Lean not only seeks to make the product look good. It also focuses on making sure that nothing is wrong with the quality or the building of the process itself. Therefore the value stream goes all the way through the process required to make the product. Any process started should go all the way to completion. This is a real problem in many companies, where projects often begin, then get pushed aside because of a small problem.

Example: A firm is doing a research project regarding the building of an airstrip. But the project gets held up, pushed aside, or slowed down by reformatting or other changes. This can result in a lot of waste, extra costs, and loss of time. Although it's impossible to reach perfection, a lean firm always tries to be better than its competitors.

Lean Advantages

- Plans for production that can be in varying lot sizes for customer needs
- Integrates product life cycle through supply, production, customer use, and disposal

- Synthesizes new process ideas across all levels
- Eliminates command and control with pull system priorities
- Builds an innovative, knowledgeable team

Lot size, or order quantity, is the amount of a particular item that is ordered from the plant or a supplier. For non-production operations, the word “production” can be replaced with “customer needs,” and “varying lot sizes” can be replaced with “various volumes.” The main idea is to find and use techniques that can take out the waste, improve the speed, and clean up the operation. Focus is also on adding total quality or sigma quality, which means to eliminate as much variation as possible from the processes. In production, “pull system” refers to the production of items only as demanded for use, or the replacement of those taken for use. *Pull system* also has a material control context, where it refers to the withdrawal of inventory as demanded by the operations using the inventory. Material is not issued until a signal comes from the user. Finally, pull system has an application in distribution, focusing on a system for replenishing field warehouse inventories, wherein replenishment decisions are made at the field warehouse itself, and not at the central warehouse or plant. An innovative, knowledgeable team is needed to lead and decide what the focus of the improvement should be.

Lean Management Impacts:

- Suppliers
- Internal Manufacturing
- Distribution and Logistics
- Customers

Lean management integrates into one speedy pull system with no wasteful buffering inventories between each process.

In lean manufacturing or in lean management, we are looking for the ability to pull all products through the system, rather than push them. Pull means that you get them when they’re needed. Push means that you push them whether or not they’re needed--which will create waste. Lean means that all managers should be trying to make sure that there is no wasteful buffering of inventories, paper, paperwork, files or other things waiting to be worked on, simply because one worker in a process is faster than the next one in line. That’s the problem to solve. Any thing going through the system needs to move consistently, and it needs to be pulled into the system from suppliers, all the way to customers.

How Customers are Affected

- The shortest lead time wins orders
- Planning time is shorter for customers
- Inventories are lower by default
- Suppliers take the risk, but with more certainty
- Costs are reduced as waste is reduced in the buyer-supplier interfaces

The term "lead time" means the span of time required to perform an activity. In a logistics context, it refers to the time between recognition of the need for an order and the receipt of goods. Individual components of lead time can include order preparation time, queue time, move or transportation time, and receiving and inspection time. There can be manufacturing lead time as well as purchasing lead time.

Competitive Issues

- Someone else is doing lean, too.
- Customers' expectations are higher.
- Process differentiation is also a competitive advantage.
- More orders are won based on lean performance.

A company striving to improve its operations has to beat its competitors, who are all striving toward the same goal. The firm that achieves successful improvement first, and can maintain being first, becomes a winner. However, the winning firm must continuously apply the lean process. This means that it must always remain vigilant for the next piece of waste, loss, or excess cost.

Lean Business Results

Figure 1-1

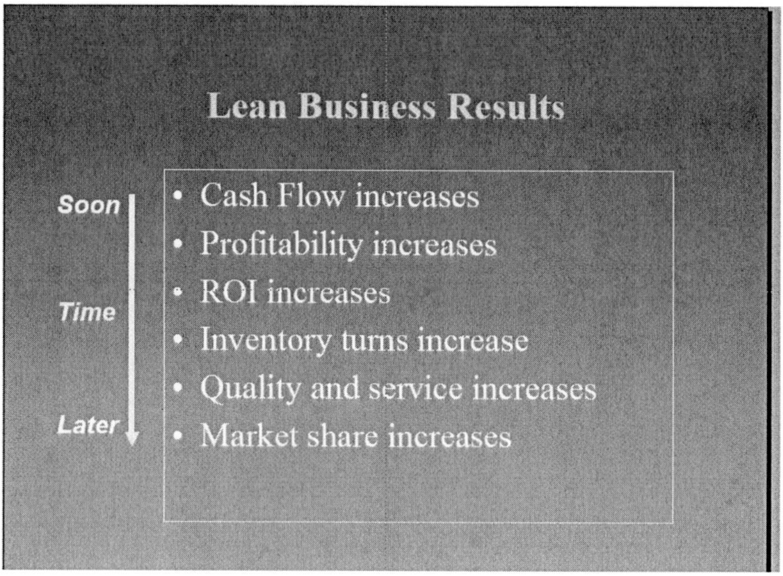

The benefits of lean can easily be seen in organizations or companies engaged in making a profit. Yet, lean is equally beneficial to non-profit entities that are operating from a budget. For either type of organization, reducing costs via lean is more effective than cutting and slashing arbitrary costs, which often ends in failure. The results of lean are quite easy to see, because they should show up in profit or enhanced operations of the company's business. Cash flow increase means that now there is more available cash than there was before you did the lean process.

Example: If, before lean, a worker used to handle something five times, and now he only has to handle it once, this means that he has essentially cut out four-fifths of the time that it took for his step in the process. If this could be applied to large numbers of workers, then the time for all labor related to that process might be reduced by four-fifths. Even if the reduction was only limited to one-half or one-forth of the original cost, the leaning would have made an improvement. Cash flow can be evident almost immediately, as opposed to many of the other results, which take more take time to see, e.g., at the end of accounting cycles.

Example: If you can reduce the amount of time spent on a process, you may reduce the need for a few workers or not need to hire as many to replace people who leave. This results in a quick, visible payroll cost reduction—and immediate cash. There are, of course, exceptions.

Example: A company in Montreal had a printer at the far end of a room, which was used by a lot of workers. Over the period of a year, they had to walk 725 miles, without adding value to their work. Applying lean, the managers installed a few printers, localized, so they could take all of that cost and waste out of the business. The cost was very minimal per printer, but there was a lot of benefit from reducing the walking. But the results couldn't be seen until they reached the end of the year, when it was evident that they hadn't hired any new employees, which would have increased costs. Instead, they got more productivity out of the same people.

Profitability increases any time you can find a way to take waste, loss, cost, or time out of the process as it is passing through the business. In manufacturing companies, the three major elements of labor, material, and overhead can all be leaned. In service industries, there are still materials to some extent, as well as overhead. There is also a selling expense, a general administrative expense, and officers, etc., that can be leaned to increase profit.

Inventory turns increase with lean. For example, if it takes six months for inventory to pass through and you can reduce that to three months, then the money you had tied up in it is now released, being turned back into usable cash.

Return on investment (ROI) increases with lean. A company buys materials and sells its product in order to get something back for it besides what the firm put into it. This return occurs in time, either sooner or later. Soon means that as soon as something happens, the return should show up. But certain things show up later in the time continuum, such as when inventory turns increase.

Quality and service increase with lean. Service means that the company provides the quality product to the customer and solves any problems in a timely manner.

Market share increases with lean. This takes a longer period of time to see, because it takes a while for a company to build an image and to educate the public on how good their product is.

Order Winners and Order Qualifiers

Visualize the entire organization, a major product area, or simply a segment of your operation. Whatever makes people buy from your company instead of a competitor's is called an order winner. It could be:

- Higher quality
- Lower Price
- Better delivery
- More availability

If any of the above isn't what makes people choose your product over what your competitors offer, then that aspect is called an order qualifier. For instance, even if delivery isn't what makes them buy your product, they still expect it to be delivered on time.

Order Winners: Those competitive characteristics that the *customer sees* as the key reason why they buy.
Order Qualifiers: Those competitive characteristics that the *customer sees* as expected from any supplier.

Competitive Advantages – Exercise

Figure 1-2

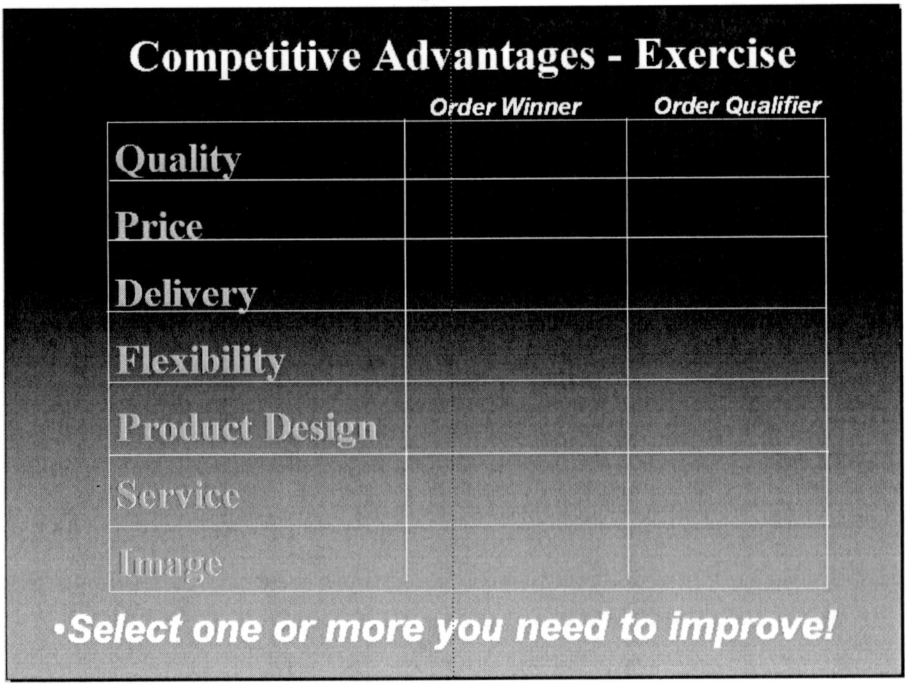

Make a table, such as the chart in Figure 1-2. From among the seven competitive advantage elements, put a check mark in the slot where each is either an order winner or an order qualifier.

Example: One of the companies that I worked with was a division of 3M. The product that they made typically had a three-week delivery time. When we finished applying lean techniques to the operations, we found that we could deliver that same product in about three or four hours. And, of course, the cost of the process was reduced too. This was a wonderful order winner for the company, because people used to have to wait a long time to get these products, and they needed them much faster than the marketplace was providing. So their company built its reputation on better delivery, better stocking programs, etc.

Example: It is possible for a company's image or brand name to be an order winner. For instance, people may buy more products made by 3M than from one of its competitors because of their confidence in the name. This trust in the image is, of course, based upon the other six competitive advantages. An organization can only enhance its image by successfully developing those other six, and this usually has to occur over time. Federal

Express is also an order winner brand, although its delivery speed is largely involved in that image.

Chapter 1 Homework Assignment

Using the results of the previous Competitive Advantages Exercise, that is, the specific advantages that would move your company forward, conduct the following activities at your work site:

1. Identify three wasteful, foolish, time consuming activities that directly affect one specific advantage you selected from your exercise.
2. Identify one thing you could do that would reduce one or all of these wasteful events.

Example: A woman in one of my classes did this assignment at her company. She studied all of the existing operations, collecting information, recording data, and examining the processes of that business. A supervisor noticed and asked her why she was asking so many questions. When she explained that it was a homework assignment for her class, the supervisor prohibited her from doing any further study of their operations. When she came back to class, we all laughed at the idea that she got banned for trying to find ways to improve production. She had uncovered visual evidence of how some people were not doing their work correctly, but the management was more afraid that they were all going to get into trouble, because she had revealed the defects and deficiencies.

Example: I worked with a paint company that was well known all around the U.S. and the world. They had a problem filling their five-gallon cans with paint; these cans accounted for a lot of sales volume and profit. It simply took applying some of the examples that have been discussed here (and some we will cover later) to set up a better structure for filling their five-gallon cans of paint. The problem was that they had so disorganized and mishandled the structure of the filling process, that anybody could look at it and see how to clean it up. And that's exactly what happened. The general manager, and the key production operations manager who was in my class, simply applied these lean examination techniques. They became famous throughout their entire company as improvement gurus, just from starting with this type of exercise.

Example from Dennis Fisher (with a solution): A company in Toronto. had a packaging machine, and it seemed that they couldn't quite get the requisite amount of materials to keep the machine at maximum volume output. By asking lean-oriented questions, we found that it was simply because some manager had decided to do everything in lots of tens. That meant ten cases, ten pallets, and ten of everything else. He considered this very simple, but it actually added a lot of unnecessary time and waste to the system, so that the materials couldn't get into the machine on time. They had everything they needed to be successful, but this debilitating and unnecessary rule had superseded everything else. So, they just fixed it by reducing the amount of material provided to match only the amount needed.

Chapter 1 Quiz

1. Value is added by inventory turns reductions. True or false?
Answer: False. Customers pulling their inventory, product design for manufacturing, and small lot sizes add value.

2. Which of the following will result from the optimized use of resources defined in lean?
   - A. Customer satisfaction
   - B. Waste
   - C. More Time
   - D. Better morale

Answer: A is correct.

3. Which of the following is NOT included in lean values?
   - A. The value of a product
   - B. The value stream of a company
   - C. The flow of values without interruption
   - D. The values that are pulled to the customers

Answer: B is correct.

4. Flexibility positively impacts competitive advantages for a company. True or false?
Answer: True.

5. Which of the following is usually the first indication that a Lean implementation is working?

A. Better Return on Investment
B. Greater market share
C. Better delivery from suppliers
D. Better cash flow

Answer: D is correct.

6. Which of the seven competitive advantages are mostly controlled by operations?

A. Quality
B. Product Design
C. Delivery
D. Price

Answer: C is correct.

Chapter 2: Lean Tools and Methods

1. Identify your type of manufacturing environment.

The first step in applying lean is to understand the nature of your organization's environment. Different environments require different questions in the search for ways to lean the processes and operations. This section will introduce you to the different environments and will help you identify the elements of your organization that may differ from other types of operations. You will be given a list of typical differences between comparative manufacturing models. Then you will:
1) Identify those elements most closely related to your operations.
2) Identify the type-model company you are most like.
3) Select the proper test from the Just-In-Time (JIT) Self Tests in Chapter 5, based upon your environment.

2. Take the Just-In-Time Self Test.

The questions relate to operating results or actions within your company. Either take the test yourself as an individual, or give it to the whole company. You or your company will be given a set of questions to which you will answer with a simple "yes" or "no." Be as objective as possible by viewing your operations, people, policies, processes, and business practices from a distance. Avoid ego, pride, or bias in your answers.

3. Score the test.

Two scoring tools will help you to determine A, B, C, and D class ratings for yourselves and your company. Then compare them to the expert-based Just-In-Time performance-model in Chapter 6. This model is based on research from many companies, industry experts, and previous test results. To simplify the rating process, associated score and rating sheets for several type-models are provided. At the end of this step, you will have accomplished one or both of the following activities:

- One: You will have scored your individual test by totaling your responses to the JIT Self Test and compared the results to the JIT expert-based model.
- Two: you will have scored your company by giving the JIT Self Test to your company as a whole and scored the results using the JIT Self Test scoring and rating sheets.

Once you finish your scoring and rating sheets, you will discover whether you are a Class A, B, C, or D lean (JIT) organization. Everyone should be informed what the rating was if they have taken the test.

4. Evaluate the results.
The evaluation of the results will help you focus on the shortcomings that were highlighted in the Just-In-Time Self Test and stimulate action for improvement. You will identify your shortcomings by listing the "no" responses from the Just-In-Time Self Test and selecting which areas have shortcomings that need to be overcome.

5. Read the chapters that detail the application of lean and other internationally proven improvement techniques.

Chapter 3: Identifying Your Lean Environment

Different types of organizations and companies will have different environments of operation. You will need help in identifying the elements of your environment that may differ from other types of lean operations. This section gives you a list of typical differences and comparative operational models. You can then:

1. Check off those elements most closely related to you.
2. Compare the number of differing elements to a set of standard manufacturing models.
3. Determine your environment from the type-models provided.
4. Select which test to take from Chapter 5.

The following is a list of various types of manufacturing type-models. Select one that most closely fits your company or operation. Those who most fit the repetitive list should consider Just In Time as soon as possible, or they will lose competitive advantage. Remember, even service-oriented and non-profit organizations can benefit from learning how to lean their operations.

REPETITIVE

The repetitive manufacturing environment type produces discrete units, planned, and executed to a schedule. It usually involves relatively high speeds and volumes. Material tends to move in a continuous flow during production, but different items may be produced sequentially within that flow.

Those who fit the repetitive list are most directly related to all of the elements of the full self-test. Essentially all of the activities in a repetitive environment can use JIT.

Here are identifying aspects of the repetitive environment:

- Make-to-stock or assemble-to-order products
- Controllable work patterns
- Medium to high volume
- Repetitive patterns
- Defects less than 2 percent
- Assembly operations
- Easy to understand processes
- Predictable patterns
- Planned by rates
- Driven by daily schedules, not by work orders
- Fixed routings
- Process costing

- Dispersed machinery formed into lines

Examples of the repetitive environment include:

- Food processing
- Electronics products
- Autos
- Consumer products
- Paint
- Computers

JOB SHOP

The job shop environment type is typically a make-to-order manufacturing plant. Products are made in intermittent sequences as defined by specific customer orders. A make-to-order product is one that is finished after receipt of a customer order.

Those who fit the job shop list may still be able to use lean or JIT techniques well but are limited in some applications. It is the repetitive activities that cause most waste and that continuous improvement can improve most easily. Many of the activities in a job shop environment may be repetitive and by definition can use lean/JIT for improvement.

Here are identifying aspects of the job shop environment:

- All products are unique made-to-order items
- Plans and controls are by orders or lots
- Use of work orders is unavoidable
- Variable routings exist between products
- Job costing is done by work order
- Multipurpose machinery is grouped together
- Low volumes are usual

Examples of the job shop environment include:

- R&D shops
- Sheet metal
- Molding
- Airplanes
- Custom woodworking
- Printing

PROCESS FLOW

The process flow environment type is a production approach with minimal interruptions in actual processing in any one production run. It also has minimal interruptions in processing between production runs of similar products. Queue time is virtually eliminated by integrating the moving of the product into the actual operation of the resource performing the work.

This environment has production flow in a continuous process. Process industries are already in much of the JIT flow because there is little inventory between workstations. But other waste reduction issues will apply to their support activities.

Here are identifying aspects of the process flow environment:

- All products are made to stock or distribution
- Planning done by shift or period rates
- Fixed routings for all products
- Fixed, dedicated equipment
- Distinct line orientation for most products
- High volumes are usual

Examples of the process flow environment include:

- Pharmaceuticals
- Oil refining
- Chemicals
- Steel
- Cement
- Textiles
- Carpets
- Beer

PROJECT PRODUCTION

The project production environment usually involves special custom building of large units or the grouping of things like ships or housing projects.

Here are identifying aspects of the project production environment:

- Make-to-order or assemble to order products
- Planned by project or major assembly
- Usually low volume
- Semi-variable routers
- Usually a large stationary project
- Heavy use of subcontracting

Examples of the project production environment include:

- Shipbuilding
- Construction
- Specialty chemicals
- Supercollider–superconductor

There are many similarities and commonalities between all of the type-models listed above. Any of the questions in the Just In Time Self-Test that are tied to the following list of similarities will apply to all types-models.

Similarities or common issues for all type-models are:
People involvement
Customer satisfaction
Workplace organization
Training and cross-training
Supplier management
Total quality management[1]
Management support
Problem solving
Preventive or productive maintenance
Set-up time reduction[2]
Cycle time reduction[3]
Signaling systems
Inventory reduction
Throughput improvement[4]
Operating expense reduction
People involvement and team building.
Storage and floor space reduction.
Measurement systems.

[1]**Total quality management (TQM)** is an approach encompassing all phases of an organization that attempts to insure quality in all things, to ensure that no defective data, processes, or parts are produced in any department. The basic elements include statistical quality control, process control, quality at the source, group problem solving, employee involvement, customer satisfaction, team building, and continuous improvement.

[2]**Setup** refers to the process of changing dies or other parts of a machine to product a new part or product. Setup costs are those associated with a setup or changeover. Setup time is the time required for a specific machine, line, or work center to convert from the production of one specific item to another. This is typically measured from the last good part until the next (new) good part.

[3]**Cycle time** has two meanings.

(1) In industrial engineering, it means the time between completion of two discrete units of production. For example, the cycle time of motors assembled at a rate of 120 per hour would be 30 seconds, or one every half minute.
(2) In materials management, it refers to the length of time from when material enters a production facility until it exits. Cycle time is also known as throughput time.

[4]**Throughput** means the total volume of production, results, or actions through a facility or department, machine center, work cell, plant, or network of plants.

UNIQUE DIFFERENCES

Some unique differences need to be addressed for each environment type or model. The following list identifies questions in the Just In Time Self Test that may not apply to the specific type-model you might be working with. Be aware that most companies usually have elements of more than one type within their operations. If this is the case for you, don't exclude the question from your list. The following list is only intended to make the test less confusing for different environment types. These questions have been removed from the self-test, and a separate test is provided in Chapter 5 for each type.

Please note that the following list is for convenience only. After you have taken the test you may want to see which questions were eliminated from your test. Then, you can use this list:

Job Shop

Question 19	Question 34
Question 22	Question 39
Question 24	Question 51
Question 25	Question 58
Question 29	

Flow Shop

Question 26

Project

Question 18 Question 24
Question 19 Question 25
Question 20 Question 39
Question 21 Question 51
Question 23 Question 58

AFTER TAKING THE SELF-TEST

After completing the self-test, go to Chapter 6 and score yourself on the scoring and rating sheets that are designed for your environment type or model. Before continuing, one other issue that must be addressed is company size. Many people taking the Just-In-Time Self Test will be from small companies. Some of the materials in this course make reference to resources, staff, and team sizes that would be too large in scope for a small company. However, many of the principles of lean can also be tailored to address the needs of small companies who seek to improve their operations.

Chapter 4: The Lean Self Test

This chapter is designed to provide you with the generic list of questions about the operating results or actions within your companies. When you take the actual test in Chapter 5, you will be given a set of questions, which you will answer with a simple "yes" or "no." If there is substantial activity or effort going on for an item, then answer "yes." If no real effort or practice exists, answer "no." This is important to remember, because some of the questions may not be answerable with a distinct "yes" or "no." If you are not aware of any activity by your company on a particular question, then answer "no." You must answer every question.

It is imperative that you act as objective observers: viewing your operations, people, policies, processes, and business practices from a distance. Be careful to avoid ego, pride, or bias in your answers—particularly if you are tied in some way to the activities being questioned. Answer the questions by placing a check mark or "x" in the yes or no column provided.

After reading through the generic test in this chapter, be sure you have selected the correct test from Chapter 5, based on your type of company as defined in Chapter 3. The list of questions here in chapter 4 is the master list of all questions that apply to a typical JIT repetitive type-model.

The environment type-specific questionnaires in Chapter 5 have had some of the questions removed to match to their business environment. The following questions are the master list of all questions on the Just-In-Time Self Test. And again, you will be asked to respond as objectively as possible to each of the following elements of Just-In-Time.

Education and People

1. Management supports and participates in employee involvement programs that demonstrate trust, delegate authority, and allow autonomous decision-making.

2. A continuous and formal training program is in place that includes new employee indoctrination, skills development, cross training, manufacturing principles, and JIT concepts for all employees.

3. Middle management and supervisors have been reduced and reorganized to support JIT.

4. Key managers, support personnel, and operators have been trained in Just In Time practices.

5. Cross-training programs have been implemented with skills tracking and evaluations.

6. Compensation and rewards for employees are based on both employee flexibility and team contribution.

7. Department or team problem-solving groups meet regularly to address and solve quality and flow problems throughout all departments.

8. All associated functional departments (e.g., engineering, purchasing, marketing, and accounting) are part of problem-resolution teams.

9. Management responds to employee ideas and feeds back their responses immediately.

Quality Management

10. Management exhibits consistent support for quality procedures.

11. Inspection sequences have mostly been eliminated and quality is part of the individual operator's responsibility.

12. Quality control departments have been replaced with process audit and operator training functions.

13. Early warning statistical quality control tools are in place and are used to monitor and control quality at critical points in the process.

14. Quality errors are repaired or prevented at the source where they occur.

15. Fail-safe (poka-yoke) devices are installed at most locations where recurring human quality errors typically occur.

16. Work areas are consistently clean, organized, and free of unnecessary materials and equipment.

17. The majority of incoming materials are certified or source inspected at the suppliers.

18. Supplier quality certification and performance rating pro-grams are in place and are continuously monitored.

Factory Flow

19. Transportation networks consistently deliver mixed loads from local and long distance sources.

20. Standardized containers with exact quantities are used between supplier and plant for over 50 percent of the volume parts.

21. Weekly or daily delivery of 80 percent or more of production materials are made to the plant and directly to the production line points of use.

22. Supplier deliveries are scheduled by the production processes demand for parts.

23. Standard containers hold exact and consistent quantities and are maintained throughout the shop.

24. Production build-and-pull quantities are calculated to support only average daily demand.

25. Shop schedules, dispatching, work orders, and expediting have been eliminated and priorities are defined by shift schedules and quantities.

26. Parts are only produced as required by demand and are built in quantities approaching one.

27. Labor is not "kept busy" by building product when not needed at the next operation.

<u>Production Processes</u>

28. Production lines are grouped into product family (group technology) cells or lines.

29. Processes support flexible mixed model runs with minimum material handling.

30. Manufacturing is actively involved in product and process design improvement for quality and ability to be produced.

31. Production parts have been designed to facilitate fast changeover.

32. Tooling and fixtures are available when setups and jobs begin.

33. Rapid setups are established (less than 10 minutes) for most machines and lines.

34. Cycle times of each workstation, cell, or line are matched to upstream and downstream times.

35. Manufacturing processes have been reoriented to eliminate material handling.

36. Process problems are identified and visibly signaled immediately on discovery.

37. Manufacturing engineering is located in the production area and is immediately available for problem resolution.

38. Scheduled preventive maintenance is considered an important part of production performance.

Master Planning

39. Daily rate and level schedules are used and meet due dates.

40. MRP is used for demand planning, customer committing, supplier schedules, and supplier capacity planning.

41. Management participates in the planning and re-planning process and commits to a realistic capacity level.

42. Marketing promotes the demonstrated benefits of Just-In-Time to customers.

43. Production rates exactly equal demand rates, or production quantities equal demand quantities.

44. Customer on time delivery rate is 98-plus percent as committed.

Purchasing

45. Key volume suppliers are local.

46. Single-source suppliers make up greater than 50 percent of all suppliers.

47. The number of active suppliers has been reduced substantially by 50

percent or more.

48. Buyers and suppliers are rated by supplier quality, delivery, and ongoing improvement.

49. Frequent multi-department contacts are made between suppliers and your plant.

50. Most paperwork, material handling, transportation, and quality waste have been eliminated between supplier and plant.

51. Delivery lead time for most parts range from one day to one week.

Data Integrity

52. Inventory record accuracy is 98-plus percent or better for both stockrooms and point of use storage.

53. Bills of material accuracy 99-plus percent or better for costing needs and post deduct inventory.

54. Bills of materials flattened—structured with two or less levels in production.

55. Routing detail, methods, or assembly instructions are accurately defined and maintained by timely process flow changes.

56. Clearly defined engineering standards for costing.

57. Shipment forecast variation is plus or minus 10 percent or less by product family in the current time period.

58. Accounting systems and controls have been redesigned to work in a JIT environment.

Results

59. Operational measurements with both targets and tolerances are in place and reviewed daily by management and employees.

60. Overall manufacturing process cycle time and throughput lead times are reduced.

61. Production floor space has been substantially reduced.

62. Work-in-process inventories are continuously reducing.

63. Substantial increases in productivity or shipments per employee.

64. Substantially reduced operating expense.

65. Overall cost of quality is continually reducing.

66. Stockroom inventories are continuously reducing.

67. Substantially increased inventory turns.

68. On-time customer delivery is continuously increasing for both line-fill and order-fill rate.

Chapter 5: The Lean Self Test By Environment Type

The Lean Self Test - Repetitive

The Lean Self Test - Repetitive	Management Group
This questionnaire is a list of questions about repetitive manufacturing operating activities, results, or business practices within your companies. Answer each question with simple "yes" or "no" responses. If there is a substantial activity or effort going on in your company for an item, then answer "yes." If no real effort or practice exists, answer "no." This is important to remember because some of the questions may not be able to be answered with a distinct "yes" or "no." If you are not aware of any activity by your company on a particular question, answer it "no." You must answer every question.	
You must act as objective observers, viewing your operations, people, policies, processes, and business practices from a distance. Be careful to avoid ego, pride, or bias in your answers, particularly if you are tied in some way to the activities being questioned. Answer the questions by placing an "X" in the "yes" or "no" columns provided next to each question.	

Education and People		Yes	No
1. Management supports and participates in employee involvement programs that demonstrate trust, delegate authority, and allow autonomous decision making.			
2. A continuous and formal training program is in place that includes new employee indoctrination, skills development, cross training, manufacturing principles, and JIT concepts for all employees.			
3. Middle management and supervisors have been reduced and reorganized to support JIT.			
4. Key managers, support personnel, and operators have been trained in Just-In-Time practices.			
5. Cross-training programs have been implemented with skills tracking and evaluations.			
6. Compensation and rewards for employees are based on both employee flexibility and team contribution.			
7. Department or team problem-solving groups meet regularly to address and solve quality and flow problems throughout all departments.			
8. All associated functional departments (e.g., engineering, purchasing, marketing and accounting) are part of problem-resolution teams.			
9. Management responds to employee ideas and feeds back their responses immediately.			
PAGE TOTAL			

Quality Management	Yes	No
10. Management exhibits consistent support for quality procedures.		
11. Inspection sequences have mostly been eliminated and quality is part of the individual operator's responsibility.		
12. Quality control departments have been replaced with process audit and operator training functions.		
13. Early warning statistical quality control tools are in place and are used to monitor and control quality at critical points in the process.		
14. Quality errors are repaired or prevented at the source where they occur.		
15. Fail-safe (poka-yoke) devices are installed at most locations where recurring human quality errors typically occur.		
16. Work areas are consistently clean, organized, and free of unnecessary materials and equipment.		
17. The majority of incoming materials are certified or source inspected at the suppliers.		
18. Supplier quality certification and performance rating programs are in place and are continuously monitored.		
PAGE TOTAL		

Factory Flow		Yes	No
19. Transportation networks consistently deliver mixed loads from local and long distance sources.			
20. Standardized containers with exact quantities are used between supplier and plant for over 50 percent of the volume parts.			
21. Weekly or daily delivery of 80 percent or more of production materials are made to the plant and directly to the production line points of use.			
22. Supplier deliveries are scheduled by the production processes demand for parts.			
23. Standard containers hold exact and consistent quantities and are maintained throughout the shop.			
24. Production build-and-pull quantities are calculated to support only average daily demand.			
25. Shop schedules, dispatching, work orders, and expediting have been eliminated and priorities are defined by shift schedules and quantities.			
26. Parts are only produced as required by demand and are built in quantities approaching one.			
27. Labor is not "kept busy" by building product when not needed at the next operation.			
PAGE TOTAL			

Production Processes		**Yes**	**No**
28. Production lines are grouped into product family (group technology) cells or lines.			
29. Processes support flexible mixed model runs with minimum material handling.			
30. Manufacturing is actively involved in product and process design improvement for quality and ability to be produced.			
31. Production parts have been designed to facilitate fast changeover.			
32. Tooling and fixtures are available when setups and jobs begin.			
33. Rapid setups are established (less than 10 minutes) for most machines and lines.			
34. Cycle times of each workstation, cell, or line are matched to upstream and downstream times.			
35. Manufacturing processes have been reoriented to eliminate material handling.			
36. Process problems are identified and visibly signaled immediately on discovery.			
37. Manufacturing engineering is located in the production area and is immediately available for problem resolution.			
38. Scheduled preventive maintenance is considered an important part of production performance.			
PAGE TOTAL			

Master Planning	Yes	No
39. Daily rate and level schedules are used and meet due dates.		
40. MRP is used for demand planning, customer committing, supplier schedules, and supplier capacity planning.		
41. Management participates in the planning and re-planning process and commits to a realistic capacity level.		
42. Marketing promotes the demonstrated benefits of Just In Time to customers.		
43. Production rates exactly equal demand rates, or production quantities equal demand quantities.		
44. Customer on time delivery rate is 98-plus percent as committed.		
PAGE TOTAL		

Purchasing	Yes	No
45. Key volume suppliers are local.		
46. Single-source suppliers make up greater than 50 percent of all suppliers.		
47. The number of active suppliers has been reduced substantially—by 50 percent or more.		
48. Buyers and suppliers are rated by supplier quality, delivery, and ongoing improvement.		
49. Frequent multi-department contacts are made between suppliers and your plant.		
50. Most paperwork, material handling, transportation, and quality waste has been eliminated between supplier and plant.		
51. Delivery lead time for most parts range from one day to one week.		
PAGE TOTAL		

Data Integrity		Yes	No
52. Inventory record accuracy is 98-plus percent or better for both stockrooms and point of use storage.			
53. Bills of material accuracy 99-plus percent or better for costing needs and post deduct inventory.			
54. Bills of materials flattened—structured with two or less levels in production.			
55. Routing detail, methods, or assembly instructions are accurately defined and maintained by timely process flow changes.			
56. Clearly defined engineering standards for costing.			
57. Shipment forecast variation is plus or minus 10 percent or less by product family in the current time period.			
58. Accounting systems and controls have been redesigned to work in a JIT environment.			
PAGE TOTAL			

Results	Yes	No
59. Operational measurements with both targets and tolerances are in place and reviewed daily by management and employees.		
60. Overall manufacturing process cycle time and throughput lead times are reduced.		
61. Production floor space has been substantially reduced.		
62. Work-in-process inventories are continuously reducing.		
63. Substantial increases in productivity or shipments per employee.		
64. Substantially reduced operating expense.		
65. Overall cost of quality is continually reducing.		
66. Stockroom inventories are continuously reducing.		
67. Substantially increased inventory turns.		
68. On-time customer delivery is continuously increasing for both line-fill and order-fill rate.		
PAGE TOTAL		

TEST TOTAL		

The Lean Self Test - Job Shop

The Lean Self Test – Job Shop Management Group
This questionnaire is a list of questions about repetitive manufacturing operating activities, results, or business practices within your companies. Answer each question with simple "yes" or "no" responses. If there is a substantial activity or effort going on in your company for an item, then answer "yes." If no real effort or practice exists, answer "no." This is important to remember because some of the questions may not be able to be answered with a distinct "yes" or "no." If you are not aware of any activity by your company on a particular question, answer it "no." You must answer every question.
You must act as objective observers, viewing your operations, people, policies, processes, and business practices from a distance. Be careful to avoid ego, pride, or bias in your answers, particularly if you are tied in some way to the activities being questioned. Answer the questions by placing an "X" in the "yes" or "no" columns provided next to each question.

Education and People	Yes	No
1. Management supports and participates in employee involvement programs that demonstrate trust, delegate authority, and allow autonomous decision making.		
2. A continuous and formal training program is in place that includes new employee indoctrination, skills development, cross training, manufacturing principles, and JIT concepts for all employees.		
3. Middle management and supervisors have been reduced and reorganized to support JIT.		
4. Key managers, support personnel, and operators have been trained in Just In Time practices.		
5. Cross-training programs have been implemented with skills tracking and evaluations.		
6. Compensation and rewards for employees are based on both employee flexibility and team contribution.		
7. Department or team problem-solving groups meet regularly to address and solve quality and flow problems throughout all departments.		
8. All associated functional departments (e.g., engineering, purchasing, marketing and accounting) are part of problem-resolution teams.		
9. Management responds to employee ideas and feeds back their responses immediately.		
PAGE TOTAL		

Quality Management		Yes	No
10. Management exhibits consistent support for quality procedures.			
11. Inspection sequences have mostly been eliminated and quality is part of the individual operator's responsibility.			
12. Quality control departments have been replaced with process audit and operator training functions.			
13. Early warning statistical quality control tools are in place and are used to monitor and control quality at critical points in the process.			
14. Quality errors are repaired or prevented at the source where they occur.			
15. Fail-safe (poka-yoke) devices are installed at most locations where recurring human quality errors typically occur.			
16. Work areas are consistently clean, organized, and free of unnecessary materials and equipment.			
17. The majority of incoming materials are certified or source inspected at the suppliers.			
18. Supplier quality certification and performance rating programs are in place and are continuously monitored.			
PAGE TOTAL			

Factory Flow		**Yes**	**No**
19.			
20. Standardized containers with exact quantities are used between supplier and plant for over 50 percent of the volume parts.			
21. Weekly or daily delivery of 80 percent or more of production materials are made to the plant and directly to the production line points of use.			
22.			
23. Standard containers hold exact and consistent quantities and are maintained throughout the shop.			
24.			
25.			
26. Parts are only produced as required by demand and are built in quantities approaching one.			
27. Labor is not "kept busy" by building product when not needed at the next operation.			
PAGE TOTAL			

Production Processes		Yes	No
28. Production lines are grouped into product family (group technology) cells or lines.			
29.			
30. Manufacturing is actively involved in product and process design improvement for quality and ability to be produced.			
31. Production parts have been designed to facilitate fast changeover.			
32. Tooling and fixtures are available when setups and jobs begin.			
33. Rapid setups are established (less than 10 minutes) for most machines and lines.			
34.			
35. Manufacturing processes have been reoriented to eliminate material handling.			
36. Process problems are identified and visibly signaled immediately on discovery.			
37. Manufacturing engineering is located in the production area and is immediately available for problem resolution.			
38. Scheduled preventive maintenance is considered an important part of production performance.			
PAGE TOTAL			

Master Planning		**Yes**	**No**
39.			
40. MRP is used for demand planning, customer committing, supplier schedules, and supplier capacity planning.			
41. Management participates in the planning and re-planning process and commits to a realistic capacity level.			
42. Marketing promotes the demonstrated benefits of Just In Time to customers.			
43. Production rates exactly equal demand rates, or production quantities equal demand quantities.			
44. Customer on time delivery rate is 98-plus percent as committed.			
PAGE TOTAL			

Purchasing		Yes	No
45. Key volume suppliers are local.			
46. Single-source suppliers make up greater than 50 percent of all suppliers.			
47. The number of active suppliers has been reduced substantially—by 50 percent or more.			
48. Buyers and suppliers are rated by supplier quality, delivery, and ongoing improvement.			
49. Frequent multi-department contacts are made between suppliers and your plant.			
50. Most paperwork, material handling, transportation, and quality waste has been eliminated between supplier and plant.			
51.			
PAGE TOTAL			

Data Integrity	Yes	No
52. Inventory record accuracy is 98-plus percent or better for both stockrooms and point of use storage.		
53. Bills of material accuracy 99-plus percent or better for costing needs and post deduct inventory.		
54. Bills of materials flattened—structured with two or less levels in production.		
55. Routing detail, methods, or assembly instructions are accurately defined and maintained by timely process flow changes.		
56. Clearly defined engineering standards for costing.		
57. Shipment forecast variation is plus or minus 10 percent or less by product family in the current time period.		
58.		
PAGE TOTAL		

Results	Yes	No
59. Operational measurements with both targets and tolerances are in place and reviewed daily by management and employees.		
60. Overall manufacturing process cycle time and throughput lead times are reduced.		
61. Production floor space has been substantially reduced.		
62. Work-in-process inventories are continuously reducing.		
63. Substantial increases in productivity or shipments per employee.		
64. Substantially reduced operating expense.		
65. Overall cost of quality is continually reducing.		
66. Stockroom inventories are continuously reducing.		
67. Substantially increased inventory turns.		
68. On-time customer delivery is continuously increasing for both line-fill and order-fill rate.		
PAGE TOTAL		

TEST TOTAL		

The Lean Self Test - Flow Shop

The Lean Self Test – Flow Shop	**Management Group**
This questionnaire is a list of questions about repetitive manufacturing operating activities, results, or business practices within your companies. Answer each question with simple "yes" or "no" responses. If there is a substantial activity or effort going on in your company for an item, then answer "yes." If no real effort or practice exists, answer "no." This is important to remember because some of the questions may not be able to be answered with a distinct "yes" or "no." If you are not aware of any activity by your company on a particular question, answer it "no." You must answer every question.	
You must act as objective observers, viewing your operations, people, policies, processes, and business practices from a distance. Be careful to avoid ego, pride, or bias in your answers, particularly if you are tied in some way to the activities being questioned. Answer the questions by placing an "X" in the "yes" or "no" columns provided next to each question.	

Education and People	Yes	No
1. Management supports and participates in employee involvement programs that demonstrate trust, delegate authority, and allow autonomous decision making.		
2. A continuous and formal training program is in place that includes new employee indoctrination, skills development, cross training, manufacturing principles, and JIT concepts for all employees.		
3. Middle management and supervisors have been reduced and reorganized to support JIT.		
4. Key managers, support personnel, and operators have been trained in Just In Time practices.		
5. Cross-training programs have been implemented with skills tracking and evaluations.		
6. Compensation and rewards for employees are based on both employee flexibility and team contribution.		
7. Department or team problem-solving groups meet regularly to address and solve quality and flow problems throughout all departments.		
8. All associated functional departments (e.g., engineering, purchasing, marketing and accounting) are part of problem-resolution teams.		
9. Management responds to employee ideas and feeds back their responses immediately.		
PAGE TOTAL		

Quality Management	Yes	No
10. Management exhibits consistent support for quality procedures.		
11. Inspection sequences have mostly been eliminated and quality is part of the individual operator's responsibility.		
12. Quality control departments have been replaced with process audit and operator training functions.		
13. Early warning statistical quality control tools are in place and are used to monitor and control quality at critical points in the process.		
14. Quality errors are repaired or prevented at the source where they occur.		
15. Fail-safe (poka-yoke) devices are installed at most locations where recurring human quality errors typically occur.		
16. Work areas are consistently clean, organized, and free of unnecessary materials and equipment.		
17. The majority of incoming materials are certified or source inspected at the suppliers.		
18. Supplier quality certification and performance rating programs are in place and are continuously monitored.		
PAGE TOTAL		

Factory Flow		Yes	No
19. Transportation networks consistently deliver mixed loads from local and long distance sources.			
20. Standardized containers with exact quantities are used between supplier and plant for over 50 percent of the volume parts.			
21. Weekly or daily delivery of 80 percent or more of production materials are made to the plant and directly to the production line points of use.			
22. Supplier deliveries are scheduled by the production processes demand for parts.			
23. Standard containers hold exact and consistent quantities and are maintained throughout the shop.			
24. Production build-and-pull quantities are calculated to support only average daily demand.			
25. Shop schedules, dispatching, work orders, and expediting have been eliminated and priorities are defined by shift schedules and quantities.			
26.			
27. Labor is not "kept busy" by building product when not needed at the next operation.			
PAGE TOTAL			

Production Processes		**Yes**	**No**
28. Production lines are grouped into product family (group technology) cells or lines.			
29. Processes support flexible mixed model runs with minimum material handling.			
30. Manufacturing is actively involved in product and process design improvement for quality and ability to be produced.			
31. Production parts have been designed to facilitate fast changeover.			
32. Tooling and fixtures are available when setups and jobs begin.			
33. Rapid setups are established (less than 10 minutes) for most machines and lines.			
34. Cycle times of each workstation, cell, or line are matched to upstream and downstream times.			
35. Manufacturing processes have been reoriented to eliminate material handling.			
36. Process problems are identified and visibly signaled immediately on discovery.			
37. Manufacturing engineering is located in the production area and is immediately available for problem resolution.			
38. Scheduled preventive maintenance is considered an important part of production performance.			
PAGE TOTAL			

Master Planning		Yes	No
39. Daily rate and level schedules are used and meet due dates.			
40. MRP is used for demand planning, customer committing, supplier schedules, and supplier capacity planning.			
41. Management participates in the planning and re-planning process and commits to a realistic capacity level.			
42. Marketing promotes the demonstrated benefits of Just In Time to customers.			
43. Production rates exactly equal demand rates, or production quantities equal demand quantities.			
44. Customer on time delivery rate is 98-plus percent as committed.			
PAGE TOTAL			

Purchasing		Yes	No
45. Key volume suppliers are local.			
46. Single-source suppliers make up greater than 50 percent of all suppliers.			
47. The number of active suppliers has been reduced substantially—by 50 percent or more.			
48. Buyers and suppliers are rated by supplier quality, delivery, and ongoing improvement.			
49. Frequent multi-department contacts are made between suppliers and your plant.			
50. Most paperwork, material handling, transportation, and quality waste has been eliminated between supplier and plant.			
51. Delivery lead time for most parts range from one day to one week.			
PAGE TOTAL			

Data Integrity	Yes	No
52. Inventory record accuracy is 98-plus percent or better for both stockrooms and point of use storage.		
53. Bills of material accuracy 99-plus percent or better for costing needs and post deduct inventory.		
54. Bills of materials flattened—structured with two or less levels in production.		
55. Routing detail, methods, or assembly instructions are accurately defined and maintained by timely process flow changes.		
56. Clearly defined engineering standards for costing.		
57. Shipment forecast variation is plus or minus 10 percent or less by product family in the current time period.		
58. Accounting systems and controls have been redesigned to work in a JIT environment.		
PAGE TOTAL		

Results	Yes	No
59. Operational measurements with both targets and tolerances are in place and reviewed daily by management and employees.		
60. Overall manufacturing process cycle time and throughput lead times are reduced.		
61. Production floor space has been substantially reduced.		
62. Work-in-process inventories are continuously reducing.		
63. Substantial increases in productivity or shipments per employee.		
64. Substantially reduced operating expense.		
65. Overall cost of quality is continually reducing.		
66. Stockroom inventories are continuously reducing.		
67. Substantially increased inventory turns.		
68. On-time customer delivery is continuously increasing for both line-fill and order-fill rate.		
PAGE TOTAL		

TEST TOTAL		

The Lean Self Test - Project

The Lean Self Test - Project	Management Group
This questionnaire is a list of questions about repetitive manufacturing operating activities, results, or business practices within your companies. Answer each question with simple "yes" or "no" responses. If there is a substantial activity or effort going on in your company for an item, then answer "yes." If no real effort or practice exists, answer "no." This is important to remember because some of the questions may not be able to be answered with a distinct "yes" or "no." If you are not aware of any activity by your company on a particular question, answer it "no." You must answer every question.	
You must act as objective observers, viewing your operations, people, policies, processes, and business practices from a distance. Be careful to avoid ego, pride, or bias in your answers, particularly if you are tied in some way to the activities being questioned. Answer the questions by placing an "X" in the "yes" or "no" columns provided next to each question.	

Education and People	Yes	No
1. Management supports and participates in employee involvement programs that demonstrate trust, delegate authority, and allow autonomous decision making.		
2. A continuous and formal training program is in place that includes new employee indoctrination, skills development, cross training, manufacturing principles, and JIT concepts for all employees.		
3. Middle management and supervisors have been reduced and reorganized to support JIT.		
4. Key managers, support personnel, and operators have been trained in Just In Time practices.		
5. Cross-training programs have been implemented with skills tracking and evaluations.		
6. Compensation and rewards for employees are based on both employee flexibility and team contribution.		
7. Department or team problem-solving groups meet regularly to address and solve quality and flow problems throughout all departments.		
8. All associated functional departments (e.g., engineering, purchasing, marketing and accounting) are part of problem-resolution teams.		
9. Management responds to employee ideas and feeds back their responses immediately.		
PAGE TOTAL		

Quality Management	**Yes**	**No**
10. Management exhibits consistent support for quality procedures.		
11. Inspection sequences have mostly been eliminated and quality is part of the individual operator's responsibility.		
12. Quality control departments have been replaced with process audit and operator training functions.		
13. Early warning statistical quality control tools are in place and are used to monitor and control quality at critical points in the process.		
14. Quality errors are repaired or prevented at the source where they occur.		
15. Fail-safe (poka-yoke) devices are installed at most locations where recurring human quality errors typically occur.		
16. Work areas are consistently clean, organized, and free of unnecessary materials and equipment.		
17. The majority of incoming materials are certified or source inspected at the suppliers.		
18.		
PAGE TOTAL		

Factory Flow		**Yes**	**No**
19.			
20.			
21.			
22. Supplier deliveries are scheduled by the production processes demand for parts.			
23.			
24.			
25.			
26. Parts are only produced as required by demand and are built in quantities approaching one.			
27. Labor is not "kept busy" by building product when not needed at the next operation.			
PAGE TOTAL			

Production Processes		Yes	No
28. Production lines are grouped into product family (group technology) cells or lines.			
29. Processes support flexible mixed model runs with minimum material handling.			
30. Manufacturing is actively involved in product and process design improvement for quality and ability to be produced.			
31. Production parts have been designed to facilitate fast changeover.			
32. Tooling and fixtures are available when setups and jobs begin.			
33. Rapid setups are established (less than 10 minutes) for most machines and lines.			
34. Cycle times of each workstation, cell, or line are matched to upstream and downstream times.			
35. Manufacturing processes have been reoriented to eliminate material handling.			
36. Process problems are identified and visibly signaled immediately on discovery.			
37. Manufacturing engineering is located in the production area and is immediately available for problem resolution.			
38. Scheduled preventive maintenance is considered an important part of production performance.			
PAGE TOTAL			

Master Planning		Yes	No
39.			
40. MRP is used for demand planning, customer committing, supplier schedules, and supplier capacity planning.			
41. Management participates in the planning and re-planning process and commits to a realistic capacity level.			
42. Marketing promotes the demonstrated benefits of Just In Time to customers.			
43. Production rates exactly equal demand rates, or production quantities equal demand quantities.			
44. Customer on time delivery rate is 98-plus percent as committed.			
PAGE TOTAL			

Purchasing		**Yes**	**No**
45. Key volume suppliers are local.			
46. Single-source suppliers make up greater than 50 percent of all suppliers.			
47. The number of active suppliers has been reduced substantially—by 50 percent or more.			
48. Buyers and suppliers are rated by supplier quality, delivery, and ongoing improvement.			
49. Frequent multi-department contacts are made between suppliers and your plant.			
50. Most paperwork, material handling, transportation, and quality waste has been eliminated between supplier and plant.			
51.			
PAGE TOTAL			

Data Integrity	**Yes**	**No**
52. Inventory record accuracy is 98-plus percent or better for both stockrooms and point of use storage.		
53. Bills of material accuracy 99-plus percent or better for costing needs and post deduct inventory.		
54. Bills of materials flattened—structured with two or less levels in production.		
55. Routing detail, methods, or assembly instructions are accurately defined and maintained by timely process flow changes.		
56. Clearly defined engineering standards for costing.		
57. Shipment forecast variation is plus or minus 10 percent or less by product family in the current time period.		
58.		
PAGE TOTAL		

Results		**Yes**	**No**
59. Operational measurements with both targets and tolerances are in place and reviewed daily by management and employees.			
60. Overall manufacturing process cycle time and throughput lead times are reduced.			
61. Production floor space has been substantially reduced.			
62. Work-in-process inventories are continuously reducing.			
63. Substantial increases in productivity or shipments per employee.			
64. Substantially reduced operating expense.			
65. Overall cost of quality is continually reducing.			
66. Stockroom inventories are continuously reducing.			
67. Substantially increased inventory turns.			
68. On-time customer delivery is continuously increasing for both line-fill and order-fill rate.			
PAGE TOTAL			

TEST TOTAL			

Chapter 6: Scoring the Lean Self-Test

Now that you've taken the test or have administered it to your company, two scoring tools will help you determine your lean (Just-In-Time) ratings. You can then compare yourself to the JIT rating scheme listed in this chapter. This rating scheme is based on extensive research from many companies and industry experts. Follow the instructions on each type of "self test score and rating sheets." The four sets of scoring and rating sheets are designed for each of the associated environment type or model.

1. For an individual evaluation
a. Take the appropriate Just-In-Time Self Test.
b. Total your "yes" responses to the Just-In-Time Self Test.
c. Compare your personal results to the JIT model.
d. Read the subsequent chapters.

2. For a company evaluation
a. Give the Just-In-Time Self Test to your company as a group.
b. Score the results using the self-test scoring and rating sheets.
c. Read the subsequent chapters.

Scoring & Rating Sheets - Repetitive

Figure 6-1

JIT Self Test Worksheet—Repetitive

Mgm't Level	Scoring Matrix					Level Matrix		
	1-19	20-31	32-44	45-56	57-68	4 Levels	3 Levels	2 Levels
1 Top	1	2	3	4	5		XX	XX
2 Mid	1	2	3	4	5			XX
3 Supv	1	2	3	4	5			
4 Line	1	2	3	4	5			
					Totals			

1. Total all tests from the employees. Sort the tests by management level.

2. Enter the scores from each test by management level in the scoring matrix (use a "hen scratch" like ////). For example, if the Supervisory employee's scores for seven employees were 35, 41, 29, 34, 60, 52, 44, then the numbers entered in the scoring matrix would be 1 in 20—31, 4 in 32—44, 1 in 45—56 and 1 in 57—68. Do the same for all management levels in your company.

3. Circle the box 1 through 5 that represents the highest count (hen scratches) in each organization level and enter 1, 2, 3, 4, or 5 in the Level Matrix boxes to the right under the column representing the number of management levels in your organization. Then fill in the appropriate "totals" box at the bottom of the column.

Figure 6-2

JIT Self Test Rating—Repetitive

Management Levels:	*4 Levels*	*3 Levels*	*2 Levels*	
	Worksheet Score Ranges			***CLASS***
Post the total score from the rating worksheet in the appropriate box	16–20	13–15	9–10	**A**
	12–15	10–12	7–8	**B**
	8–11	6–9	5–6	**C**
	4–7	3–5	2–4	**D**

1. Identify the column representing the number of management levels in your organization.

2. Post the total from the Rating Worksheet in the box representing the range that contains your score.

3. Your JIT Self-Test class rating will be in the right hand column!

Figure 6-3

Individual Rating Scheme—Repetitive		
Use this rating scheme if only one individual is being tested.		
Score		
Class A	57 to 68	Well implemented! Don't quit now!
Class B	45 to 56	Some missing elements! Check which items are answered "no" and begin analysis. Prioritize items by cost-benefit then by shortest time to implement.
Class C	32 to 44	Halfway there! There are a number of major procedural problems to be solved. More training may be needed. Do not let perceived benefits from JIT slow your attention to process flows and WIP reductions. Investigate support groups.
Class D	20 to 31	You are making some headway! Considerable change to the flows and planning processes will be difficult to overcome. Management support may be lacking or misunderstood. Training in both applications and concepts are an absolute necessity. Support groups will be having real trouble adjusting.
	Below 19	This could be any company. Many of the basic activities for JIT are also necessary for any well-operating firm. The JIT philosophy will require a refocusing of old planning habits, quality control disciplines, demand management, data accuracy, and manufacturing process changes.

Scoring & Rating Sheets - Job Shop

Figure 6-4

JIT Self Test Worksheet—Job Shop

Mgm't Level	Scoring Matrix					Level Matrix		
	1–19	*20–31*	*32–44*	*45–56*	*57–68*	*4 Levels*	*3 Levels*	*2 Levels*
1 Top	1	2	3	4	5		XX	XX
2 Mid	1	2	3	4	5			XX
3 Supv	1	2	3	4	5			
1 Line	1	2	3	4	5			
					Totals			

1. Total all tests from the employees. Sort the tests by management level.

2. Enter the scores from each test by management level in the scoring matrix (use a "hen scratch" like ////). For example, if the Supervisory employee's scores for seven employees were 35, 41, 29, 34, 60, 52, 44, then the numbers entered in the scoring matrix would be 1 in 20-31, 4 in 32-44, 1 in 45-56 and 1 in 57-68. Do the same for all management levels in your company.

3. Circle the box 1 through 5 that represents the highest count (hen scratches) in each organization level and enter 1, 2, 3, 4, or 5 in the Level Matrix boxes to the right under the column representing the number of management levels in your organization. Then fill in the appropriate "totals" box at the bottom of the column.

Figure 6-5

JIT Self Test Rating—Job Shop

Management Levels:	*4 Levels*	*3 Levels*	*2 Levels*	*CLASS*
	Worksheet Score Ranges			
Post the total score from the rating worksheet in the appropriate box	16–20	13–15	9–10	A
	12–15	10–12	7–8	B
	8–11	6–9	5–6	C
	4–7	3–5	2–4	D

1. Identify the column representing the number of management levels in your organization.
2. Post the total from the Rating Worksheet in the box representing the range that contains your score.
3. Your JIT Self-Test class rating will be in the right hand column!

Figure 6-6

Individual Rating Scheme—Job Shop		
Use this rating scheme if only one individual is being tested.		
Score		
Class A	57 to 68	Well implemented! Don't quit now!
Class B	45 to 56	Some missing elements! Check which items are answered "no" and begin analysis. Prioritize items by cost-benefit then by shortest time to implement.
Class C	32 to 44	Halfway there! There are a number of major procedural problems to be solved. More training may be needed. Do not let perceived benefits from JIT slow your attention to process flows and WIP reductions. Investigate support groups.
Class D	20 to 31	You are making some headway! Considerable change to the flows and planning processes will be difficult to overcome. Management support may be lacking or misunderstood. Training in both applications and concepts are an absolute necessity. Support groups will be having real trouble adjusting.
	Below 19	This could be any company. Many of the basic activities for JTI are also necessary for any well-operating firm. The JIT philosophy will require a refocusing of old planning habits, quality control disciplines, demand management, data accuracy, and manufacturing process changes.

Scoring & Rating Sheets - Flow Shop

Figure 6-7

JIT Self Test Worksheet—Flow Shop

Mgm't Level	Scoring Matrix 1–19	20–31	32–44	45–56	57–68	Level Matrix 4 Levels	3 Levels	2 Levels
1 Top	1 ___	2 ___	3 ___	4 ___	5 ___	☐	XX	XX
2 Mid	1 ___	2 ___	3 ___	4 ___	5 ___	☐	☐	XX
3 Supv	1 ___	2 ___	3 ___	4 ___	5 ___	☐	☐	☐
1 Line	1 ___	2 ___	3 ___	4 ___	5 ___	☐	☐	☐
					Totals	☐	☐	☐

1. Total all tests from the employees. Sort the tests by management level.

2. Enter the scores from each test by management level in the scoring matrix (use a "hen scratch" like ////). For example, if the Supervisory employee's scores for seven employees were 35, 41, 29, 34, 60, 52, 44, then the numbers entered in the scoring matrix would be 1 in 20-31, 4 in 32-44, 1 in 45-56 and 1 in 57-68. Do the same for all management levels in your company.

3. Circle the box 1 through 5 that represents the highest count (hen scratches) in each organization level and enter 1, 2, 3, 4, or 5 in the Level Matrix boxes to the right under the column representing the number of management levels in your organization. Then fill in the appropriate "totals" box at the bottom of the column.

Figure 6-8

JIT Self Test Rating—Flow Shop

Management Levels:	*4 Levels*	*3 Levels*	*2 Levels*	
	Worksheet Score Ranges			*CLASS*
Post the total score from the rating worksheet in the appropriate box	16–20	13–15	9–10	A
	12–15	10–12	7–8	B
	8–11	6–9	5–6	C
	4–7	3–5	2–4	D

1. Identify the column representing the number of management levels in your organization.
2. Post the total from the Rating Worksheet in the box representing the range that contains your score.
3. Your JTT Self-Test class rating will be in the right hand column!

Figure 6-9

Individual Rating Scheme—Flow Shop		
Use this rating scheme if only one individual is being tested.		
Score		
Class A	57 to 68	Well implemented! Don't quit now!
Class B	45 to 56	Some missing elements! Check which items are answered "no" and begin analysis. Prioritize items by cost-benefit then by shortest time to implement.
Class C	32 to 44	Halfway there! There are a number of major procedural problems to be solved. More training may be needed. Do not let perceived benefits from JIT slow your attention to process flows and WIP reductions. Investigate support groups.
Class D	20 to 31	You are making some headway! Considerable change to the flows and planning processes will be difficult to overcome. Management support may be lacking or misunderstood. Training in both applications and concepts are an absolute necessity. Support groups will be having real trouble adjusting.
	Below 19	This could be any company. Many of the basic activities for JIT are also necessary for any well-operating firm. The JIT philosophy will require a refocusing of old planning habits, quality control disciplines, demand management, data accuracy, and manufacturing process changes.

Scoring & Rating Sheets – Project

Figure 6-10

JIT Self Test Worksheet—Project

Mgm't Level	*Scoring Matrix*					*Level Matrix*		
	1–19	20–31	32–44	45–56	57–68	4 Levels	3 Levels	2 Levels
1 Top	1	2	3	4	5		XX	XX
2 Mid	1	2	3	4	5			XX
3 Supv	1	2	3	4	5			
1 Line	1	2	3	4	5			
					Totals			

1. Total all tests from the employees. Sort the tests by management level.

2. Enter the scores from each test by management level in the scoring matrix (use a "hen scratch" like////). For example, if the Supervisory employee's scores for seven employees were 35, 41, 29, 34, 60, 52, 44, then the numbers entered in the scoring matrix would be 1 in 20-31, 4 in 32-44, 1 in 45-56 and 1 in 57-68. Do the same for all management levels in your company.

3. Circle the box 1 through 5 that represents the highest count (hen scratches) in each organization level and enter 1, 2, 3, 4, or 5 in the Level Matrix boxes to the right under the column representing the number of management levels in your organization. Then fill in the appropriate "totals" box at the bottom of the column.

Figure 6-11

JIT Self Test Rating—Project

Management Levels:	*4 Levels*	*3 Levels*	*2 Levels*	
	Worksheet Score Ranges			*CLASS*
Post the total score from the rating worksheet in the appropriate box	16–20	13–15	9–10	A
	12–15	10–12	7–8	B
	8–11	6–9	5–6	C
	4–7	3–5	2–4	D

1. Identify the column representing the number of management levels in your organization.

2. Post the total from the Rating Worksheet in the box representing the range that contains your score.

3. Your JIT Self-Test class rating will be in the right hand column!

Figure 6-12

Individual Rating Scheme—Project		
Use this rating scheme if only one individual is being tested.		
Score		
Class A	57 to 68	Well implemented! Don't quit now!
Class B	45 to 56	Some missing elements! Check which items are answered "no" and begin analysis. Prioritize items by cost-benefit then by shortest time to implement.
Class C	32 to 44	Halfway there! There are a number of major procedural problems to be solved. More training may be needed. Do not let perceived benefits from JIT slow your attention to process flows and WIP reductions. Investigate support groups.
Class D	20 to 31	You are making some headway! Considerable change to the flows and planning processes will be difficult to overcome. Management support may be lacking or misunderstood. Training in both applications and concepts are an absolute necessity. Support groups will be having real trouble adjusting.
	Below 19	This could be any company. Many of the basic activities for JIT are also necessary for any well-operating firm. The JIT philosophy will require a refocusing of old planning habits, quality control disciplines, demand management, data accuracy, and manufacturing process changes.

Chapter 7: Accelerating the Supply Chain

Accelerating the supply chain means speeding up the flow from the supplier to the customer. A big project may take six months to pass the flow through.

Example: The flow from supply to customer in the manufacturing of a typical aluminum can is about 365 days. This is from the time the (bauxite) ore inventory is extracted from the ground, through the many manufacturing stages, until finally an actual aluminum can product is completely made. This takes a calendar year, although most people would think that it would only take a few weeks or months.

Learning Objectives

- Identify the flow throughout your supply chain
- Design for the customer's customer
- Design for the supplier's supplier
- Define how to interface with suppliers

Supply Chain Flow

For most (80-95%) of all of the supply chain time, work in progress is simply sitting in piles between each of the stages that it takes to make the product. In the aluminum can example, the supply chain was shown to be as high as 365 days to make a simple soda pop can. But it would only take a matter of weeks if you could just take the first part, run it through, have it made, go to the next location, and then the next, and so on, until the can was completed. There's actually only about two hours of time spent making the product; yet it takes a whole year to get it through the process, because there are piles upon piles of inventory.

In Figure 7-1, lead time setback refers to the delay caused by all of the steps of a process or an event through which a product must pass, such as engineering design changes, new model development, or purchasing contracts. Almost all of the work in almost every industry or market is done in a series of processes—each done in sequence, one after the other. Step levels are very clear if they're in a bill of material for physical engineering. However, in many cases, a level could simply be some intermediate point of the process, as production starts from somewhere uphill, then flows down to the next level in the process, then down to the next level, and down to the next, etc., until finally the product is completed, installed, offered, or served to whoever the customer is.

Figure 7-1

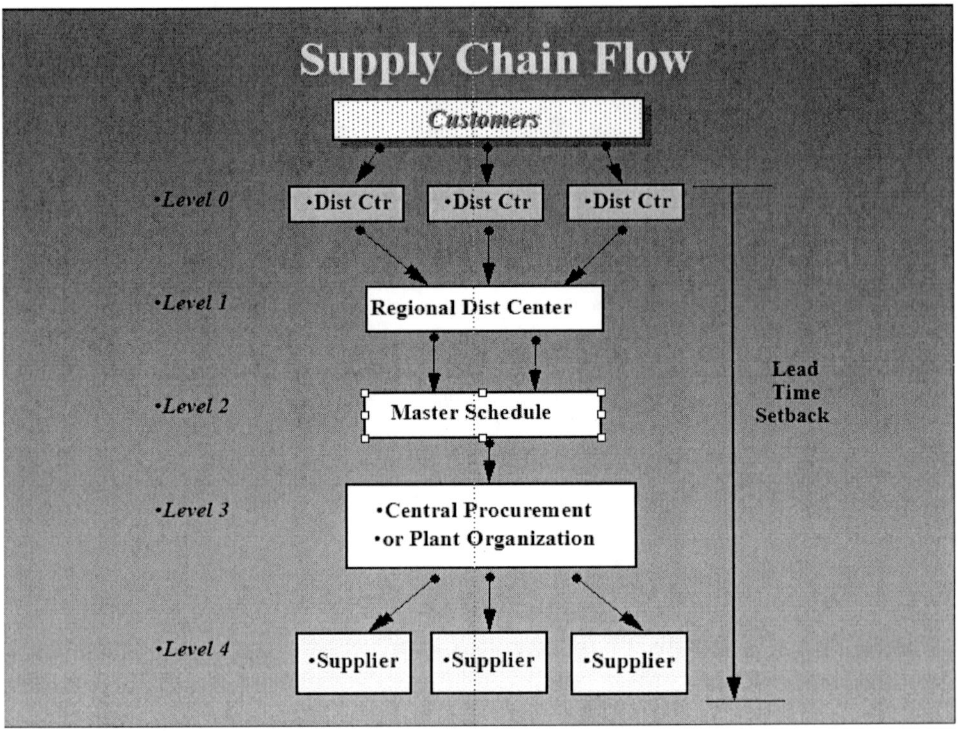

Rapid Response to Customers

Benefits from Lean Engineering, parts count reduction, and process focus include:

- Reduced throughput cycle time
- Reduced quality defects and resultant shortages
- Reduced non-value adding activities: Receiving, scheduling, purchasing, storing, space, headcount, administration, overhead, etc.
- Reduced engineering time on maintenance: Specifications, supplier management, documentation

Every business, regardless of what type, usually starts at a designated time, work is performed for a period of hours, and then it stops at a designated time. Next, maybe a second group comes in and repeats this sequence. Even if we don't think about it, everything is time-sequenced in our work. The challenge with leaning the supply chain flow lies with how well you can project, forecast, or schedule that work to be done.

How can you determine whether a supply chain flow from one step to the next, to the next, and to the next is as lean as possible? The goal is to look for that which can be done to increase the speed in the entire process. But it's difficult to know where you're going or how long any given step in the process will be if you don't have some sense of what the schedule is. In lots of companies, that schedule might be only in somebody's head, and not formally stated or recorded. In other companies there may be a schedule, but it's plagued by errors, e.g., being so overloaded that it is impossible to be met. Leaning (accelerating) the supply chain often improves many businesses right away.

Minimum Forecast and Schedules

A forecast is an estimate of future demand. It can be:

- Determined by mathematical means using historical data
- Created subjectively by using estimates from informal sources
- Established to represent a combination of both techniques

A simple way of doing scheduling begins, of course, with a forecast. From there, that forecast becomes a schedule—if it is achievable, or "doable". This is the key area to focus on. For the schedule to be considered doable means that it is attainable within the period of time defined.

Scenario: A number of years ago, Disney World's Epcott Center was supposed to open in Florida on a scheduled date. At that time, Disney was called WEBMAYPO (Walter E. Disney and Mary Poppins), and their management had a development concept called Imagineering. Combining imagination and engineering, they had great ideas, but they were so busy Imagineering, that it was hard for them to ever keep a schedule. So we came in and simply worked on what needed to happen for results. We forced everyone to agree to do whatever Imagineering they had to do on schedule. And it's amazing how well it happened. We were the cause of Epcott Center opening on time–simply by changing the means by which they were scheduling.

- As throughput speed is increased, the need for detailed forecasts diminishes.
- Suppliers are pulled closer to customer needs.
- Schedules and pulls become more stable, based on longer agreements.
- Accuracy increases as cycle time decreases and lot sizes get smaller.

If you can shorten the time to delivery to customers, then your ability to see the future is not nearly as complex, because you only need to see a shorter period. As you take out the waste and shorten the time between your schedule steps, then your forecasting becomes much more accurate.

Lean Flow and Supply Chain Stability

- Erratic outputs vs. production linearity are usually based on large orders or large internal production lots.
- Smaller lots mean shorter and more consistent delivery
- Pull systems from suppliers stabilize the supply chain.
- Pull systems to customers stabilize demand
- Small lots help stabilize production

Erratic outputs have often happened where people are making things in large lot quantities. The following example will illustrate the problem. Let's say that you make 100 of something, and that it takes one minute per piece to make 100 units. This means that it takes 100 minutes for it to pass through one step of the process, whatever that might be (painting, assembly, or typing), etc. Then the same 100 units have to move to (pass through to) the next location for work. Now, imagine that there are ten steps in a given location and that each takes one minute to operate on the work. And imagine that you have 100 in each location. So you have 100 minutes for the first location, 100 minutes for the next stage, 100 minutes for the next stage, etc. If you have four stages, this means 400 minutes have been expended. And for the next item after that to pass through, it will have to wait those 400 minutes to pass through.

While the quantity is there, 99 are sitting, and one is working. When one more goes away, we take the 98th one, but the 100th one is now sitting while we're working on the 99th and then the 98th, etc. So, every unit will have to wait the entire time for the batch to pass through. To lean this process, however, you could just cut the lot in half, which would reduce the wait time to 50 minutes. You would have cut your throughput time in half.

Scenario: This also happened at a 3M installation. Believing that large batches were more economic, they had lot sizes that were running at 20,000 or 40,000 units—weeks' and months' worth of supplies. The fact is that large lots are really not economic. The concept of efficiency doesn't work here. In actuality, the smallest lot possible ("smallest painful lot size to run") is the most desirable batch size. When the company cut their lot size in half, it was hardly noticed by anyone at the firm. However, the delivery to the customers was now twice as fast. When you cut the lot quantity in half, you simply cut the lead-time in half. If you cut it in half again, you've cut the lead-time by 75% -- first 50, then another 25. So, you've now reduced lead-time to pass through work by 75%. Thus leaning the supply caused major improvements in this example of lean supply.

Example of how smaller lots are better than the mass production techniques that we're all used to hearing about: Making a car at General Motors or Ford is not really mass production. It's really only a mass process, if you will. Every item going down the assembly line of an automotive manufacturer is a custom unit, made specifically to requirements. So you'll see one car going, and the next car will be a different kind and the next one still a different configuration. For example, one may have a sunroof or might have different wheels or a different kind of upholstery. Every car on those big lines is actually made one at a time—one right after the other—but a division of labor has been generated.

This takes us back to the 1800s. A division of labor was made so that you could take the car and stretch it into 500 sets of operations. But, once the first car is passed through, the next car comes through in 2-1/2 minutes, then the next car comes through in 2-1/2 minutes. So the output rate necessary for them to make a car is one every two and a half minutes. That's what mass production really is. Mass production doesn't mean making a large bunch of things at one time, but in a sequence of one only.

Here's a scenario from the television "reality" show called "Extreme Makeover," in which a crew of 100 people work simultaneously to renovate one house. The 100 people go in and completely fix up the building or house in a matter of six or seven days. This is similar to the car assembly line; it's not really mass production. This is just a massive amount of labor applied to a single task. But they sequence the tasks so that the foundation is built first, then they put up the framing. Next, they put up the roof. From there, they begin doing the internal works. Then it's painted, finished, and finally done. This all happens in sequence, but all broken down by different people, who do it in parallel.

Example of why small lots are better than the batch system: Imagine now a batch system, where the builders worked on, say, 20 houses simultaneously. But in this case they worked on just the foundations, and then they all came back and did just the frame, and then they all came back and did just the next part, and so on, until completion. This way would take a considerably longer period of time to finish one house. For instance, the concrete workers would come in pour the slab and the foundation. Then they move to the next house's foundation, and so on. And then the framers come in and they start putting in framing. When they're done, they also move to the next one, etc.

In a better method, they would all work to complete one house first before moving on to work on another house. Now, a saleable unit only takes the amount of time necessary to make one house. And it can be sold as soon as it's done. But the "mass process" method above won't allow for the sale of a house until all of the houses are finished. Not one can be sold until 20 are completed. This means that it may be three or four times longer before the output actually happens. And that's the same thing with cars. At one time, they used to do them that way, but that was long before the real evolution of autos with Henry Ford and, particularly, Dr. Ono from Toyota in Japan.

Production Linearity

Production linearity is a continuous, flowing quantity of work being done.

If something takes two minutes to be worked on, and something else takes one minute to be worked on, then, at the place where something takes two minutes to work on, you could put two workers on the job and cut the work time to one minute. And, in the place where it takes one minute to do the work, then the single worker does the work in one minute. So then, the continuous flow will be one every one minute through the cycle.

Figure 7-2

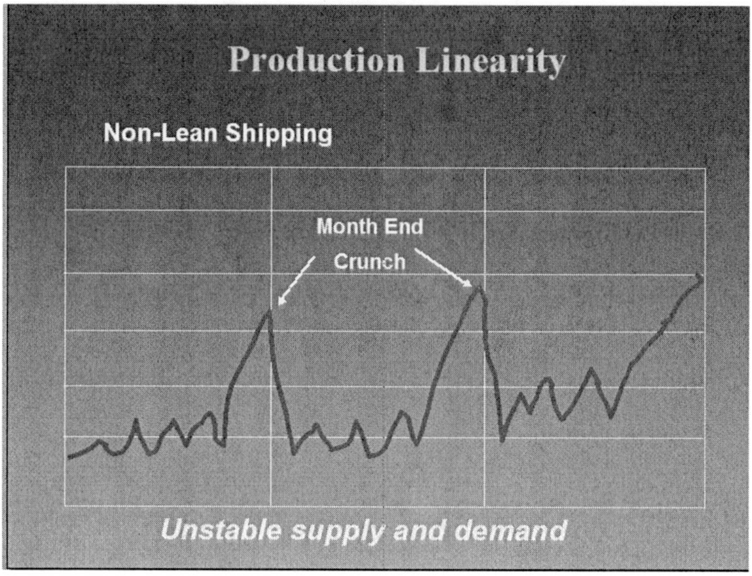

Production linearity means that things will be flowing on a constant, non-lumpy basis. Therefore, producing the smallest lot size possible can cause an increase of productivity as seen in the chart in Figure 7-2. This shows a low amount of output at the beginning of the month and then a jump at month end. It is because, at the end of the month in many companies, there is a big push to get a bunch of small quantities of products out the door to satisfy customers. But a lot of that product was being made all month in large lots, which took too long to finish. So each month, that pattern is repeated. And each month it's very wasteful, because all the inventory, time, and effort are still sitting there.

Example: In a purchasing or accounting office, they batch up all the payables every Thursday. It would be better if the payables could be processed on an ongoing basis and almost automated. But when it comes in lumps, it's very difficult to automate it, and it takes more time and effort to get checks out to customers or suppliers. Of course, suppliers charge higher rates, because they don't get paid as soon.

Figure 7-3

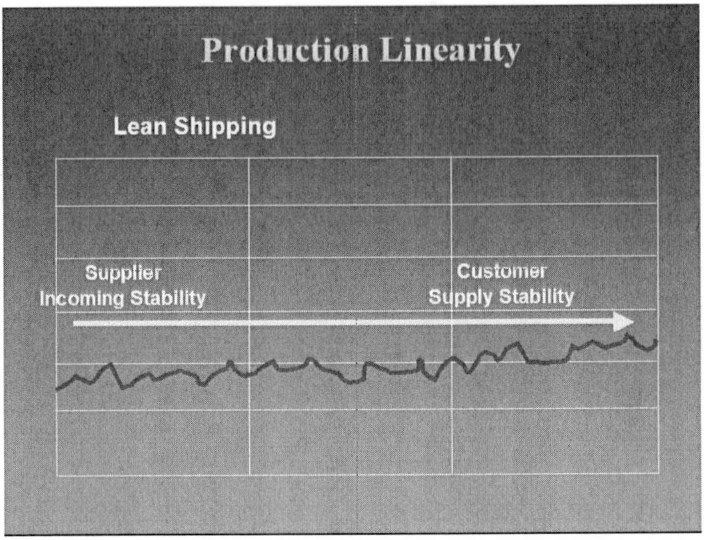

By taking production down to as small a quantity as possible by doing some each day, but progressing through from the beginning to the end, there will be no lumps, bumps, extra labor, overtime, or other additional costs when these humps and lumps occur during the monthly processes. These additional costs are referred to as "attracted" costs.

Scenario: A customer suddenly comes in and requests 1 million units of a product, immediately. If it's possible to make it available for them within the current periods, without impacting production any more than an amount determined in planning and scheduling, then you have excess or available capacity. For instance, someone comes in for a big job in the Art Department, which has ten people in it, and it's going to take two people to do that job in a short period of time. So, in order to get that job done, two other customers or two other projects are going to have to be put aside while these two people are pulled onto this new project. Obviously, it doesn't take very long before everything begins to get expedited; expediting is a self-defeating cycle. So the plan would be to charge the customer a higher fee for getting delivery in a faster period. This would cover the overtime or extra resources that have to be brought in. It makes more sense than to run the expedited production for the same cost and price as regular orders. This happens often because, although customers always want something faster, quicker, or better, you only have a certain amount of production capability or operations capability in a period.

Engineering Design for Lean

The goal here is to decrease the number of parts and the complexity of the products.

Figure 7-4 (Assy = Assembly)

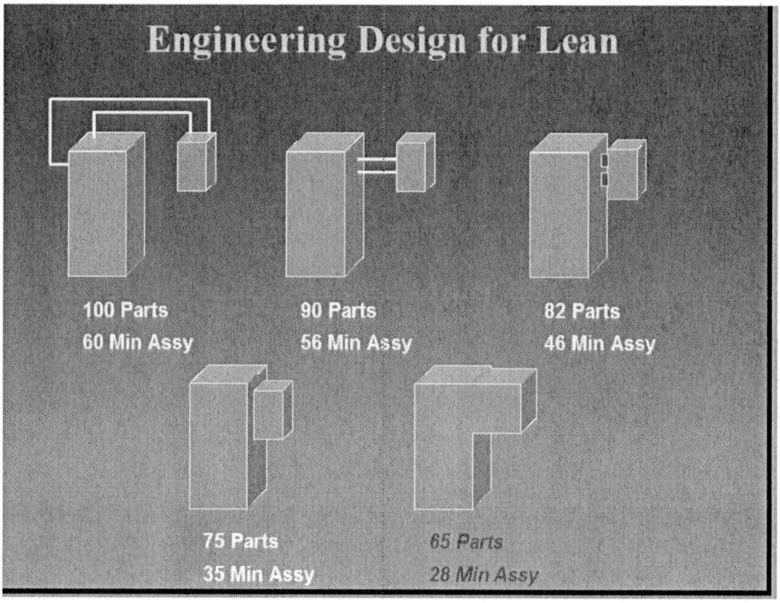

The above diagram shows an example of a product that, in its original design, could have been some tanks with controls. The actual product might be motor controllers or anything that has a control piece or a pneumatic piece, etc. attached to it. So, it has a small box with two tubes, pipes, or wires running to the big box. But we can look at the way it was designed, then go back and redesign it. We begin by asking, "Why does that thing have to be like that?" And the answer is that it doesn't have to be. We could just make it shorter and run it on one particular side of the box instead of the other side. And then you go to the next one and say,

"Instead of doing that, why don't I just put a bus bar between the two?" So there are two little bus bars there, and you just mount the box right on the bus bars, and it goes right into the other box. But, as you'll notice, the parts are now dropping from 100 parts to 82, and they will continue to drop down to a smaller number of parts when one realizes that there's no reason to have separate mountings and separate parts for the tube. As a matter of fact, it's sometimes better to just redesign the entire thing and made it all one box. Then, when you look at it, you might be able to find that there are a lot fewer parts – in this case, down to 65% of the number of parts that we had to begin with. Also, you might find that the amount of time to do the assembly could be decreased from 60 minutes to 28 minutes, yielding a 50% reduction of time.

Scenario: Here is a specific example of this concept applied to services, where we might define something in services as a part. A few years back, when I was working with Coca Cola, I ran across one of their major suppliers, who was a very good quality supplier. One of the ideas they had was to do more business with Coca Cola, and they hired me to see what I could do to help them. We found that Coca Cola had large amounts of inventory and five major warehouses around the country, providing millions of units of products for the marketplace. (This part of their business involved the equipment for the drink dispensers, not the drinks themselves.) We looked at the processes that it took to get a new machine into a new restaurant, and observed that there was a flow chart of excess effort, time, people, and complexity. So we went through a remodeling of how products could be sent out to the supplier firms that install the products. We changed their delivery scheduling, changing delivery in large lots to these major warehouses (where they sat for months or years), to delivering the products to the location in the United States through 500 installers. This potentially eliminated four of the five major warehouses that were used all across the country.

We just looked at the flow chart and the design of the system and said, "But it could be done another way if the supplier could do this." So it became a supplier's offer to the customer, and that's how the plan was adopted. In other words, the local distributor or supplier held that inventory. The local supplier in this situation was located in one place in the U.S.–on the west coast. When one was needed in Osh Kosh, Wisconsin, we would send a digital signal to send four units from back room supplies and, presto! They would be sent by the next day. We went from shipping somewhere in the area of 25 units a week to about 125 units a week. As a result, the business improved, and wasted warehousing was eliminated. Coca Cola was able to save millions, in terms of the space, handling, people, manpower, and cost of carrying inventory simply with a redesign of the flow.

Scenario: The same principle was applied to the flow of a dental office that was working with a company that made orthodontic devices. The problem with applying an orthodontic clip or a wire holder to the teeth is that an adhesive has to be mixed and catalyzed, and that catalyzing is mounted on the unit. Usually an assistant does that, and then the doctor does the work. So the assistant does his or her job, then gives it to the doctor, and the doctor puts it on the tooth. Next, they hold it for a while in ultraviolet light until it's finally stuck. That's a reasonable way for it to be done. But, a new design came out and they said, "We'll just pre-mount the adhesive on the back of the bracket, so that, when you hold it up to the tooth, you can just use ultraviolet light, and it will simply adhere to the tooth without the need for an assistant." There's a huge benefit there, in reducing the amount of manpower or personnel necessary to support the work of each of the doctors. This translated into major savings for this very popular product.

Rapid Throughput through Product Design

Product design is simply designing a product for better quality and for less handling or manipulation. In some cases, it may just be outsourcing the product so you don't do the work at all. There are many companies – and this is a key issue in today's world-class organizations – that should have been redoing what they've been doing for a long time. It isn't their expertise, really, and it's not what is referred to as a core competence. Maybe it would be better for them if they brought it in as a subassembly and then put it together with the parts with which they do have expertise. There are huge examples of this all over the world, especially with service-oriented firms that have products such as legal services. There are many places, such as law offices, that don't have their own people running the photocopy machines, doing filing, or, of course, doing their own janitorial work. There are a lot of things that are just simply outsourced as contract work. One of the core concepts behind lean manufacturing, lean operations, and lean services is either a redesign of internal product or the actual elimination of items in the process.

The following are important elements of product design:

- Part count reduction
- Combining functions of several parts
- Utilizing common part numbers across products
- Selecting assembly methods which eliminate additional parts
- Selecting designs that eliminate assembly: snap-together parts vs. screw assemblies
- Designing packaging/shipping criteria in advance

More Throughput through Product Design

- Using modular product design - Interchangeable sections of products
- Change management - Rapid product configuration at the point of demand

Another core concept in lean manufacturing, lean operations, and lean systems is finding ways to increase the throughput. Throughput means whatever is involved in the entire process, whether it's paper, orders, or products, etc. All work is tied to the flow of something through time. Even if it's a service done by a doctor or a secretary, or an item coming in, the question is still: "How fast can it pass through?"

For example, today, when you look at a construction business, it's simple. You don't buy 2 x 4s for making rafters anymore; you simple buy the entire rafter set. If you're doing flooring joists or beams, you just buy an entire pre-done joist or beam. It's already done. If you look at offices and industries, all of the electronics are available now for all back office products. Everything that you can possibly think of is either outsourced or automated. All of this gives people more time and more productivity. The greatest example is the computer. It is the greatest productivity producer today, since it has the ability to help you do ten times more work than you could before, just by using a little box on your desk.

Example: At the J. Paul Getty Museum in Los Angeles, they had a problem keeping the PC computer systems current for the hundreds of workers at the organization. Leasing was a big waste, because the computer products would come in and just sit for long periods of time before getting installed; maybe 90 days. We noticed that you could walk across the street and buy the same equipment and put it in use immediately. But the museum forced staff to go through the procurement organization or IT department. So we simply went through and redesigned the process. We set up some web pages and other communications with our suppliers. We standardized the process and allowed them to get computers of any kind, type, size, or whatever they needed in about three days.

Engineering Waste

One way to lean your organization is to ask how many of the following conditions are present in your processes. If any of them are, then you've identified symptomatic failures. This is a place to begin working towards leaning the processes.

- Engineering holds and rework
- Leaving suppliers out of design process
- Leaving customers out of design process
- Manufacturing and assembly bills
- Cleanup after product release
- Multi-tasking
- Padded estimates of completion
- Poor and inaccurate documentation

Chapter 7 Homework Assignment

1. Go to your local supermarket and ask for the store manager.
2. Explain that you are doing research on supply chain flow in America through your course.
3. Ask the manager how the flow moves through the supply system from the suppliers through distribution to his/her store.
4. Try to get an estimate of time for each step in the process.
5. Ask how long the store could stay in business at its full rate of sales if all supply were cut off one day.
6. Ask how the needs for product are transmitted to the upstream suppliers.
7. Is this market a lean operation?

The purpose of this exercise is to identify the process in a rapidly moving environment. The local supermarket is such an environment. The goal is to identify their process and how they move the inventory: from ordering it, to receiving it, to stocking it, and then tracking it out the door via bar coding and the cash register. Focus on what steps have to be passed through and the tasks used to identify how much time each step takes. You will find that, if there were a maximum full demand (such as looting during a riot or fire), it would only take about 20 minutes to empty the store's entire inventory. There is not enough food in a local supermarket to support any kind of a crisis. A typical chain will turn over product about 200 times a year. This means that inventory moves through the system in about 1-1/2 days. This is a very lean environment. That's because it's all based on this just-in-time pull mechanism. The grocery distributors are directly behind the stores and, in a matter of hours, can come to replace or replenish all inventory, either daily or every other day. If you go back to the distributors, you'll find very little inventory there either, because they get it from the major suppliers, who deliver directly to them. So, nobody has any inventory in that flow. The whole process is tightly pulling exactly the volume that's required every day. Therefore, only what will sell comes into the building.

Chapter 7 Quiz

1. What are some of the benefits of Engineering parts count reduction ? Choose all that apply.

A. Rapid response to sales and marketing
B. All of the below
C. Reduction of space required
D. Less preventive maintenance time

Answer: B is correct.

2. What is the effect on the forecast as Speed of throughput increases?

A. The forecast must be more accurate
B. The forecast must be more detailed
C. The forecast might be less detailed
D. The forecast would be for short term only

Answer: C is correct.

3. What two things would enhance Supply chain?
   A. Smaller lot size and pull systems
   B. Larger lot sizes and scheduled deliveries
   C. A fully implemented and disciplined ERP system
   D. Larger more efficient lot sizes and pull systems

Answer: A is correct

4. Which of the following would smooth or level the schedules as defined by production linearity?
   A. An accurate Master Schedule
   B. Smaller quantities of products being made
   C. A stable MRP system
   D. Pre-defined limitation of capacity

Answer: B is correct.

5. One of the lean benefits added by Engineering modular design is that of less assembly time. True or false?
Answer: True.

6. Which of the following are engineering wastes? Choose all that apply.
   A. Change notices
   B. Separate bills of material for different departments
   C. No early involvement of suppliers

Answer: A, B, & C are all correct.

Chapter 8: Speed and Internal Agility

Objectives:

- Identify waste in the typical work flows in a company
- Define the proper bills of material for lean
- Define planning and scheduling for lean
- Evaluate the impact of quality on lean systems
- List the opportunities and tools to apply lean techniques to your company

Agility Defined

Agility simply means having the ability to move quickly to follow the changing requirements of your customers and the marketplace.

Production Wastes

- Waiting in queues (lines)
- Moving materials
- Walking to get things
- Excessive time in setups
- Inspection (not testing)
- Piles of inventory
- Rework

All of the above don't add value to organization processes and, hence, are considered to be waste. Inventory items that are left idly waiting around between batches are a main source of waste. People who are just sitting around or walking a lot, moving parts or activities, and handling things multiple times are also making waste.

Example: A company had a worker who had to move back and forth between a certain location and another just behind her. But because there was large pallet blocking her direct movement, she constantly had to walk far out of her way to go around it. After an hour of discussion with management about leaning the process, they finally moved it. The worker knew it was wasteful all along, but she didn't have the authority to make the necessary change.

Inspection is one of the biggest wastes. The quality needs to be guaranteed (legally) from the supplier, hence, no time, personnel, or other resources should be spent constantly inspecting inventory or supplies. This differs from the necessary testing and series of integrity checks that have to be done. Inspection is a non-value adding activity.

Bills of Material and Lean Manufacturing

A Bill of material (BOM) is the company document that states what items go into building or producing a product. It lists all the subassemblies, intermediates, parts, and raw materials involved.

Required:

- List of items or raw materials identified by PART NUMBER
- Each item has a QUANTITY PER (assembly)
- Each item has a UNIT OF MEASURE identified

Optional:

- Drawing revision level (number or letter) for each part number
- "Make" (in-house), "buy"(outside), or "either"(in-house or buy) code
- Effectivity dates (start date and end date of authorized change)
- Cost per part, including material, labor, outside processing, burden
- Manufacturing's "ingredients list" on what to use to build the product.
- Also called a "recipe," "parts List," formula, etc.

Bill of Material

Example: A firm is making a kit of components for repairing a stove, and selling it to Sears. Five elements are required; parts such as nuts, bolts, screws, etc. It's going to require additional parts, maybe a holder, a frame, and a knob. These are all exhibited in the bill of material by having a number for each part that describes its uniqueness and then the quantity for each one.

Every bill of the material is the same. They can be as complex as 550,000 part numbers in the space shuttle at the Rockwell Space Systems Division. In the service industries, however, you can use a bill of material for calculating parts, requirements, or other parameters. Sometimes, they're called planning bills.

Figure 8-1

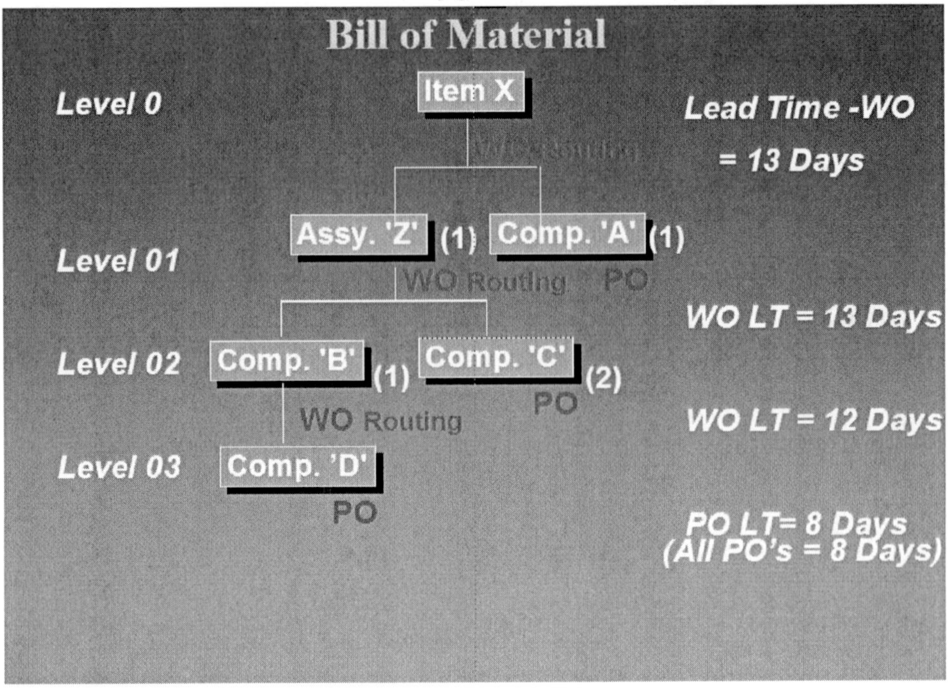

Example: Figure 8-1 shows the overall lead-time for the product of a Southern California company, which is 46 days. To lean this process, we simply issued all of the components to the final assembly area as one kit with all of the necessary parts. This allowed them to be made up and completely assembled all at the same time. We reduced the entire process, including purchasing lead-time, to 12 days. So the time it took to pass through the company went down from 46 days to 12 days, or about a 75% reduction in time. Instead of issuing multiple purchase and work orders that had to come back repeatedly to be closed, they now only needed one purchase order and one work order. The paper-handling work was cut in half, simply by using a bill of material as a way of analyzing and finding waste and loss of time. The bill of material is constructed by making a computer entry of a part number, what it's connected to, and which are the elements that are the subassembly or subcomponents.

Lean Bill of Material

Figure 8-2

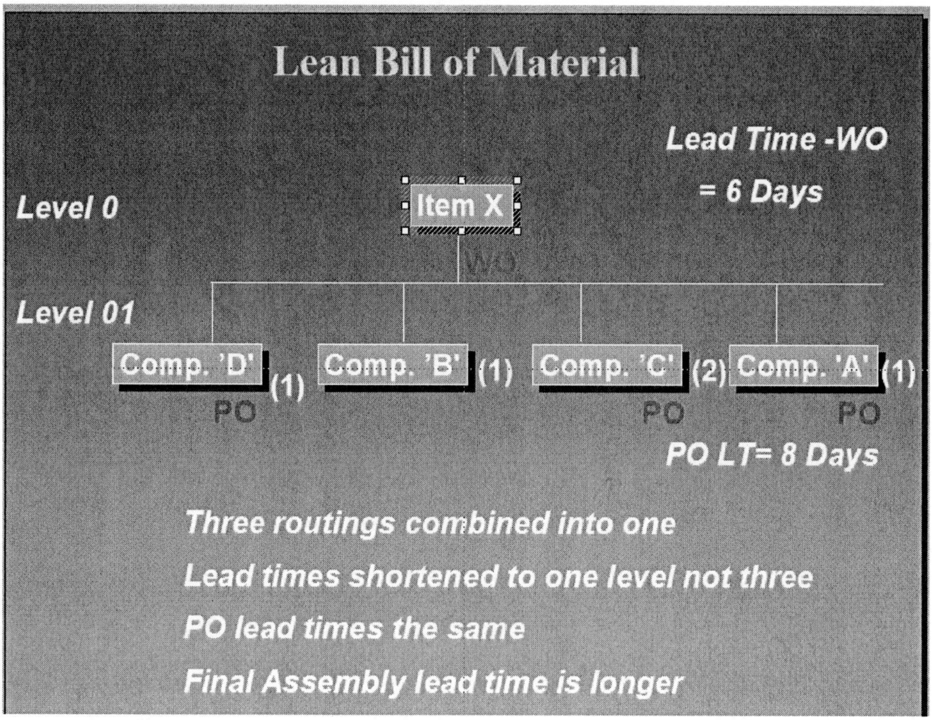

How to Convert BOM's to Lean

- Review the processes the different levels go through
- Collect the routings for each assembly
- Check if they can all be made in sequence in one line or pull flow
- Make sure the software will accommodate the restructured BOM
- Rewrite the routing for one level and the assembly instructions for each stage of the work

In the converting of the bill to make it lean, one of the tricks is simply to reorganize the assembly instructions required in each work order. The bill of material needs to have a work order, and the work order has to have a set of instructions for each step.

Flattening The BOM

Figure 8-3

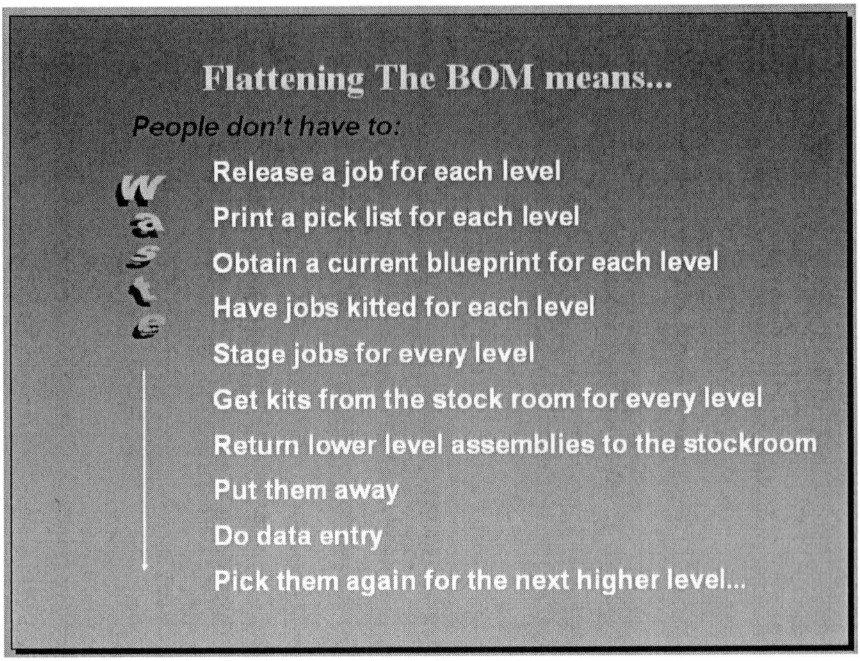

Firms such as computer repair shops often have unnecessary steps and repetition in their work order processes. There may be several necessary steps. For instance, it's a standard procedure that you always disassemble and take the motherboard out. The truth is that you don't always need to take it out. If the part needing repair just gets mounted to the motherboard, leave it there and run the tests. Companies often develop overall process definitions, not considering the fact that they become outdated and invalid.

Lean Benefits of a Flattened BOM

- Less material handling
- Less shortages
- Fewer BOMs
- Less errors and improved accuracy
- Less transactions
- Less pick lists to pick
- Less inventory

Preparing a Lean Schedule

- Identify the family group
- Identify the options

- Create the master BOM
- Create the planning bill
- Create the end item bill
- Obtain percentage of sales by option
- Calculate volume and growth by option
- Set each option in Master Schedule

The goal here is to create a schedule that integrates customer needs all the way back to the process that will fulfill it. It may go through several steps or activities on the way.

How Production is Controlled

- Production control becomes governed by pull signals
- Material is pulled by signals to suppliers
- Quality control in the hands of the value-adders
- Financial controls are undermined by the value of time

Production control is the function of directing or regulating the movement of goods through the entire manufacturing cycle; from the requisitioning of raw material to the delivery of the finished products.

Planning Bills of Material for Lean

Figure 8-4

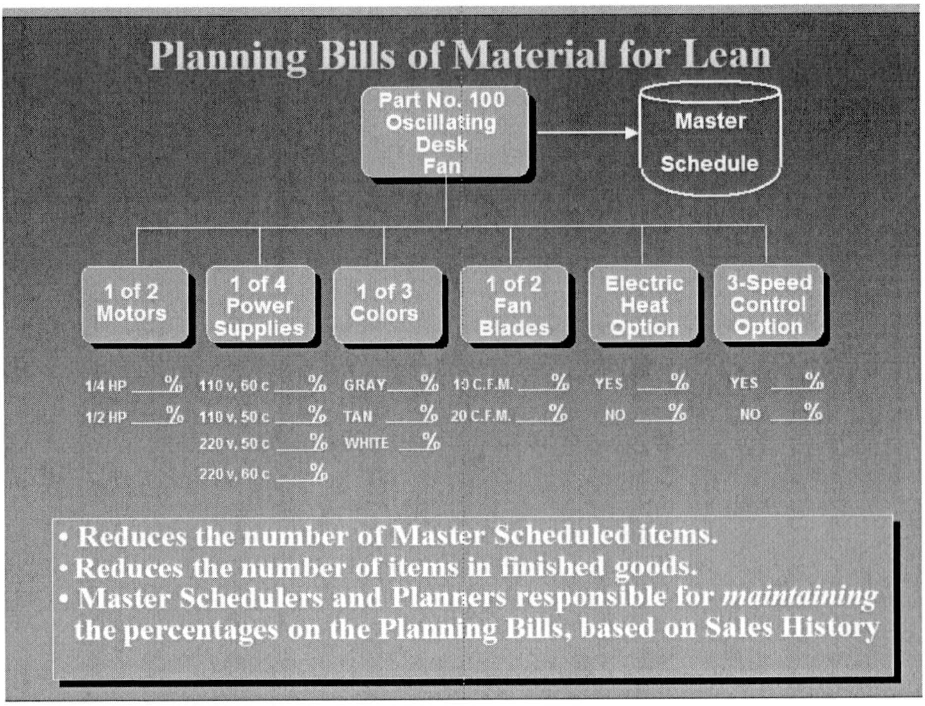

Planning bills of material is an artificial grouping of items and/or events, in bill of material format, used to facilitate master scheduling and/or material planning.

Scenario: Fig. 8-4 shows how we can break a product down into its elements. Then we take each of the elements and determine which of them are necessary to schedule, plan, and stock the product. This allows one to make what is called a planning bill. In this case the products are different types of fans, but it would be the same for different kinds of bicycles, or even automobiles. Some of the different fan models include a quarter horsepower, half horsepower, with or without a heat option, with and without a speed control, three colors, four power supplies, and two motors. Companies often just make some of each of the various types. If you take the number of motors (2) times the number of power supplies (4), that's 8. So you could have 8 configurations of just those two things. And then, on the next one, you've got three colors, so that's 24. Next, on the following one, you have 2 different kinds of fan blades, now making it 48. Then, you have a heat element or no heat element, which gives you another doubling, resulting in 96. Finally, you've got a choice of having the three-speed control option or not, so you end up with 192 different options. This means you may have to stock 192 different options in your inventories or your retail sales or whatever your operation is. However, in truth, the maximum number you'd have to supply would be a very small percent of them. There are two of the motors—quarter and half horsepower. By looking at historical usage, or maybe projected usage, you may find that you sell about 60% quarter and about 40% half horsepower motors. So that tells you that, if you had an order for 100, all you need to do is to plan on running 60 quarter and 40 half horsepower versions. You don't have to run 192 of everything. You would now have a supply close to what your demand has been or forecasted so far. The same principle applies with the number of power supplies, colors, or other configurations. In essence, there are 14 models, but you would never make a finished model. You would simply make a high level model of items to do. These high level models get pre-assembled.

Dell Computer does this. When a customer comes in for repairs, they don't actually fix the unit. They simply take out a part and replace it with a functioning one that they already have assembled. The unit is now repaired for the customer. Later, they send the failing part back to the manufacturer, so that they can replenish their stock of functioning sub-units. They overcome problems and failures with this system. Taking each of the elements and determining which of them are necessary to schedule, plan, and stock the product, they then make their planning bill.

Lean Advantages of Planning Bills

- Better response time
- Less engineering time
- Reduced costs
- Less forecast error
- Less safety stock
- Reduced number of scheduled items
- Less order entry errors

Quality and Wasteful Decisions

The following are pitfalls that need to be avoided. They are little elements that can occur with a company that does quality inspection and handling.

- Waivers without feedback and correction at the causes of failure

- MRB (Material Review Boards) ignored
- Acceptance Quality Levels (AQL) instead of PPM (Parts per Million)
- Incoming inspection
- In-process inspection
- Built-in rework in routers

If you set up waivers, pretty soon the system gets very loose, and you will end up with quality failures. This will kill your customer image. So you should have very limited waivers. As a standard, it's not a good choice. If the Material Review Board is ignored, then a blemished item can come in. Since it's unacceptable, it goes into another area, and it is stored there for later review by somebody from a technical department, typically quality or engineering. This department may eventually pass it as just having a superficial problem, such as a scratch, and they may allow the part to go into the product. The problem is that the part will not be available while it's sitting in that holding area.

AQL (Acceptance Quality Levels) means that we will accept a certain amount of failure. That means that suppliers or your own operations will allow for some unusable product. The world is moving toward a PPM (parts per million) level rather than an AQL, which is almost a percentage level. It's two out of ten or two out of 100. The PPM is essentially maybe 200 or 2,000 out of 10,000. It's a much smaller, tighter number that gives you finer control. The world is now asking for much less than 0.1% failure, and demanding that organizations achieve this much sooner. Of course, getting rid of the unnecessary inspection and doing any rework are of prime importance.

Design for Poka Yoke (Fail-Proofing)

Poka Yoke, a Japanese term, means to make a process fail-safe or foolproof. It means zero quality control, whereby the failure is simply impossible. These mistake-proofing techniques include manufacturing or setup activity, designed in a way to prevent an error from resulting in a product defect. For example, in an assembly operation, if a correct part is not used, a sensing device detects the part that was unused and shuts down the operation, thereby preventing the assembler from moving the incomplete part on to the next station or beginning another one. There are many products built this way, e.g. cameras, and computers. They all have configured chords on them that can only go into one kind of plug, so you don't—can't—cross plugs in the wrong places. Every house, building, and business has a wall plug from which it is virtually impossible to be shocked. The only reason someone may get electrocuted is because the plug or socket was not wired correctly in the first place… or because someone (maybe a child) altered the wiring. There's an entire book devoted to Poka Yoke.

Figure 8-5

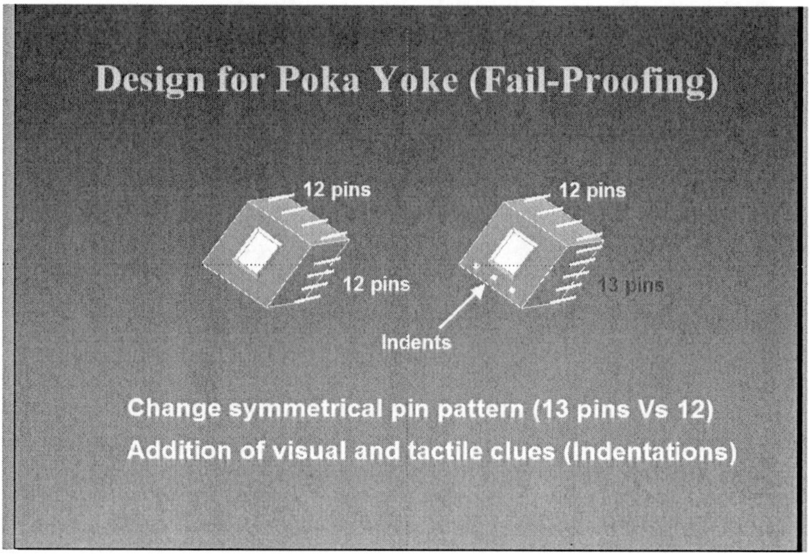

Failsafe Devices -Poka Yoke

- Bridges or jigs
- Guides or slots
- Chamfers
- Locator pins
- Micro switches

Additional failsafe devices include lens covers or power switches that automatically shut down or kill a battery

Quality Impact

Figure 8-6

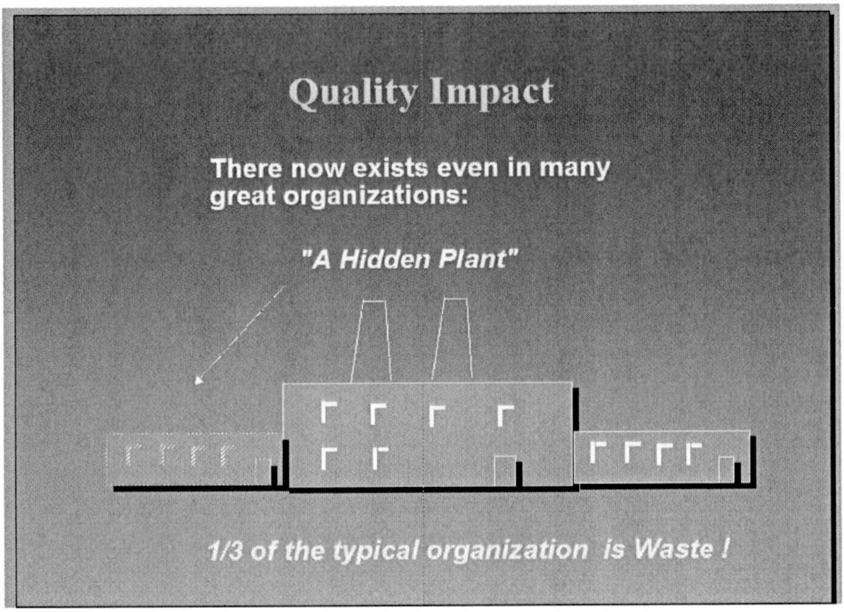

At companies around the world, about 1/3 of the operations are wasted doing everyday work. Questions for organizational managers to ask their people include:

- How much time do you spend daily in fixing, repairing, expediting, getting back to procedures, cleaning up, or doing other activities that don't really add value?
- How much time in the percent of a day is truly productive for you?

Often, managers spend a third of their time in meetings, which does not mean that they're non-productive, but often means that they're poorly productive. Another portion of their time is spent with non-productive things that occurred while they were in meetings, so 50% of their time is wasted. Figure 8-6 shows you that, if you could obtain that third back again, it would be the same as getting a whole third of a new building and all the capacity that goes into that building. It's the same, whatever the business, and it includes office spaces, equipment, and personnel. You could get 1/3 more productivity by cutting out the waste.

Customer Satisfaction Impact

Research conducted by Coca-Cola has found that:

- When people are happy with a product they will tell 4.5 other people
- When people are not happy with a product they will tell 10.5 other people
- Twice as many people will hear about a failure.
- Ten times the people will see any one failure

If your firm had 500 failures in a year and if the company grows to the point where it's up to 50,000 failures, then you have a 1% failure ratio. But, what the example tells us is that there is a lot of loss in the marketplace that you don't see when you grow. Soon, 500 failures goes up to 5,000 failures, which the whole world can now see. You're making the same product, but since there is a lot more of it in circulation, this 1% is much more visible. That's why ten times the number of people will see that failure. What wasn't a problem when the product was new can become a big problem later on.

Market Impact of Quality

Figure 8-7

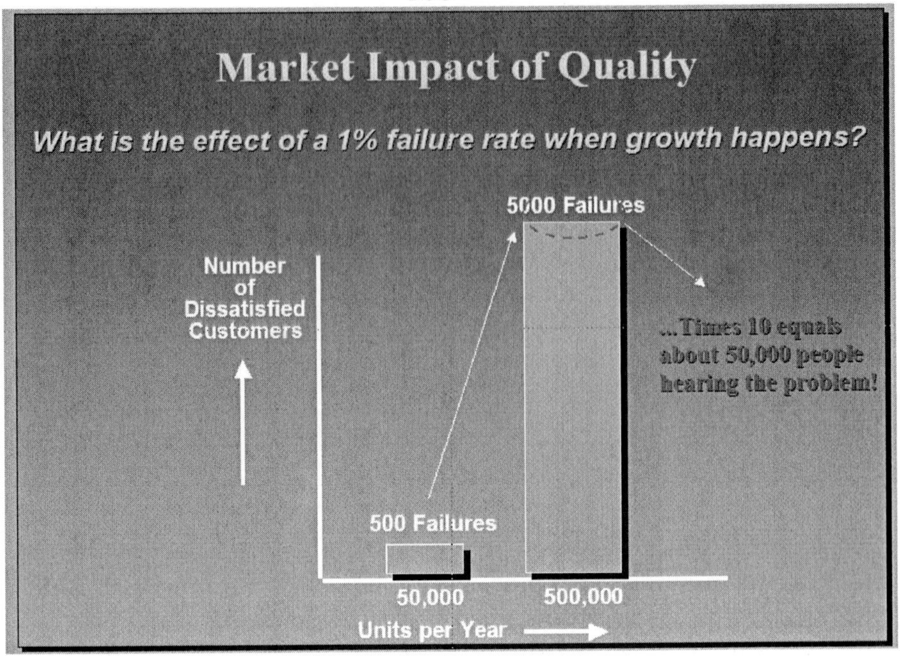

Chapter 8 Homework Assignment

1. Obtain a typical multi-level bill of material for a product your company makes.
2. Obtain the routings for each assembly in the BOM you selected.
3. Obtain the lead times for all the elements in the BOM and calculate the lead-time through the BOM.
4. Flatten the bills manually into one single level bill.
5. Restructure the router for that one level.
6. Calculate the reduction of lead-time through the BOM of this new flattened structure.

The example in Figure 8-7 is from a company called Invensys Safetran Systems. The company is 125% larger than it was four years ago. They started with 172 people, then went down to 149, not laying off or firing any workers. Staff members just quit, left for personal reasons (marriage, maternity, etc.), or died. But, even though they lost manpower, they doubled the volume of their output.

Chapter 8 Quiz

1. Rework, queues, and receiving are all considered waste in production. True or false?
Answer: True.

2. Which of the following waste is not part of Lean systems?
A. Administration waste
B. Engineering waste
C. Environmental waste
D. Production waste
Answer: C is correct.

3. The main difference between Lean and non-lean BOM's are that there are fewer work orders and fewer levels in the bills of material with lean. True or false?
Answer: True.

4. Which of the following is meant by blattening the BOM's?
A. Making the routers go away
B. Making the lead times go away
C. Making lower assemblies or fabrications go away
D. Making the picking process much faster
Answer: C is correct.

5. What is the most effective tool for the reduction of quality defects?
A. Statistical Process Control
B. Poka Yoke
C. Automated testing
D. Careful craftsmanship
Answer: B is correct.

6. What is the biggest impact of quality failure?
A. Market exposure
B. Internal Cost of Quality
C. Loss of customers
D. All of above
Answer: A is correct.

Chapter 9: Leaning the Layout

Objectives:

- Identify how to recognize waste or "muda"
- Define a layout using proper guidelines
- Check the speed through your system
- Calculate savings in both time and distance
- Note the impact of inventory on all areas

The layout is the process or the flow of the business. You lean it by eliminating Muda, which is a Japanese word for waste. Find where the waste is in detail, and then identify the speed through your system. First, you locate what kinds of things you can do to identify or calculate savings. Much of this comes from a concept called Kaizen, from a book of the same name by Masaaki Imai. This is commonly used in many companies.

Eliminating Waste (Muda)

Waste examples:

- Producing defects
- Counting
- Paperwork
- Over-production
- Expediting
- Storage
- Transportation
- Travel time

Every one of these is costing you time and money. They could also be costing you customers, new products, and extra labor. Observe your operations, and see how many of these you're doing. Identify how many different places it happens. Producing defects will occur everywhere, in everything. This is based upon how qualitative the process is. But the person involved with scheduling will be able to reveal what work is being rescheduled to correct the defects. Counting should be eliminated. If boxes come in and they're always marked exactly the same, then counting is unnecessary. If you go to a fabric store, there's a distance marker and a groove on the edge of the table to help the worker make the correct cut. So they just pull off a sheet and match to the mark, automatically measuring the cut. There's no need to use tape or any other time-wasting measures. These are fail-safe measures that eliminate counting, checking, or anything else you don't have to do in this process stage.

Paperwork, by itself, can very easily be a wasteful event. Health care is rife with that, because you have to do paperwork just for legal or regulatory purposes. Overproduction is doing more than you need to. That means, if you're typing out forms, only type out what you'll need right now. When you're done with that, move on to another task. You don't want to do a wasteful batch, because that paperwork is now going to sit with labor or time invested in it without any return. Expediting is the "rushing" or "chasing" of production or purchase orders that are needed in less than the normal lead-time. Expediting, of course, means that there's something wrong with the system, e.g., mishandling by purchasing staff, office management, or clerks. It could be that you should replace some of your processes, products, or people by leasing, contracting, or outsourcing to services that can do a more expert job. Storing inventory and transporting it more than once are both wasteful. Also, moving people from location to location creates waste.

A Core Rule: "People Don't Walk and Parts Don't Move"

The core rule underneath all this is that we simply don't want people to walk or parts to move. Parts can mean paper, forms, or sending unnecessary e-mails with parts attached, etc.

Process Oriented Layout (Job Shop)

Figure 9-1

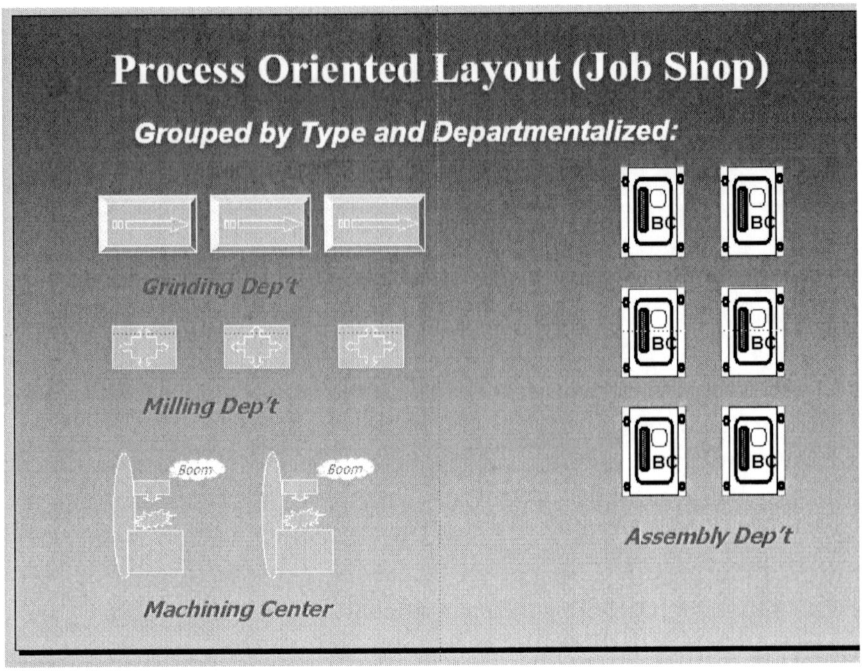

Figure 9-1 shows how to improve processes by reorganizing the elements, based upon how they are actually used in the workflow. For example, in offices or health care situations, you may have all typing done in one area. Whenever typing is needed, it's sent to that location. And then you have all photocopying in one area. The same would apply to legal and other departments. It is much better to take elements of each of those "departments" and organize them to reduce walking by workers and the movement of papers, etc.

Example. A well-known wetsuit company called Body Glove had excess inventory of their wetsuit products piling up, because they were not able sell enough before the seasonal market closed. After making a few changes to reorient the flow, we were able to reduce the time it took for the making of a wetsuit from 32 minutes down to 12 minutes. This was a two-thirds reduction in the amount of time necessary to make the product. Our reorientation also reduced the resource moving distance from hundreds and hundreds of feet to the length of a table, even dropping down through the floor directly into a warehouse. We implemented the use of one kind of sewing machine to make a straight stitch, and another kind that would do a zigzag stitch. Then the taggers and the zipper machines were lined up so that they were facing each other. This meant that, when you finished one sewing event, you moved to the next—and without having to be turned around for the next element to be sewn on. The management wouldn't do it at first, because they thought it would confuse everybody.

Product Oriented Cell (Flow Shop)

Figure 9-2

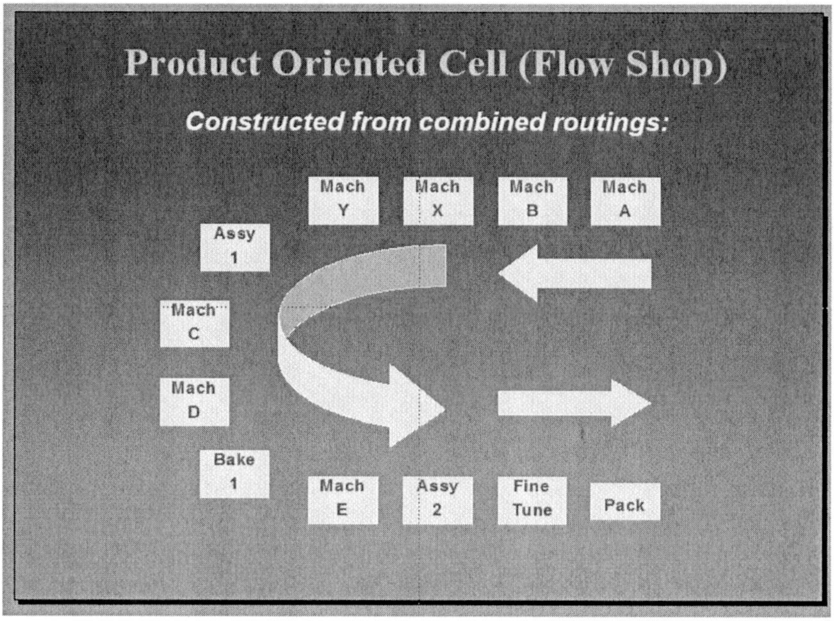

Figure 9-2 shows the way a flow would go through a cell or a cellular orientation. The machines doing the work could be anything from staplers or word processors to data entry applications. The important thing is that the work flows in a particular direction, from one desk to another desk, to the next desk, and finally to one more. Even though this flow exists, the work could be cellularized. Cellular manufacturing is a process that produces families of parts within a single line or cell of machines operated by machinists who work only within the line or cell. A work cell has all the common components in the assembly processes, including all the parts and routings that are similar. This allows the product to be made in one place instead of being moved all over the operation from place to place.

Example: On one side of the factory parking lot were a lot of the technical people and on the other side were all of the operations people. If you just stood there and watched that parking lot, you would see people all day walking a good hundred yards back and forth across the parking lot. To eliminate that tremendous amount of waste in traveling and walking, all they needed to do was move some people from here over to the other place or vice versa, so that they wouldn't have to be doing all that transiting. The term for this is *co-locate*. In Figure 9-2, we have a picture of how it would be if you formed them into a cell where work that had to get approved, checked, validated, typed, retyped, data entered, quality checked, or engineered, etc., could simply be in a cell of work. Cellular operations, cellular production, and cellular manufacturing are very common.

Example: if you go to any print shop, they'll have specific things near certain liquid containers or types of printers. If they're doing something involving a lot of color, then all of the color activities, color folding, and shearing, etc., may also be oriented into cells. The kind of work they get determines the kind of cells they should have.

Job Shop Vs. Flow Shop

Figure 9-3

Job Shop Vs. Flow Shop

Activity	Flow Shop- JIT	Job Shop- MRP
Plant Layout by:	Product	Process
Work Scheduling by:	Rate	Work Order
Routings are:	Fixed	Variable
Cost Accounting	Process	Job
Load Leveling by:	Quantity	Time
Material Handling	Standardized	Irregular

Figure 9-3 shows some of the differences between a job shop, or a shop that does a lot of unique things, and a flow shop, which simply does things repetitively. Material requirements planning (MRP) is a set of techniques that uses bills of material, inventory data, and the master production schedule to calculate requirements for materials. It makes recommendations to release replenishment orders for material. Further, since it is time phased, it makes recommendations to reschedule open orders when due dates and need dates are not in phase. Originally seen as merely a better way to order inventory, today it is thought of as primarily a scheduling technique, (i.e., a method for establishing and maintaining valid due dates—priorities) on orders. In this example, MRP is a computer output describing what jobs should be worked on. In a job shop environment, which is the right-hand column, the work is laid out by the processes, such as the picture in Figure 9-1 shown earlier with the mills in one place, grinders in the other, etc., by process. When something is made, it doesn't need each of those, but it goes back and forth between them for different pieces.

Variations can occur, as in the case of making a product, such as rubber bumpers. Your raw material is rubber, and you might use two types. Items fabricated out of the rubber are mostly made by forming or vulcanizing it.

Rubber manufacturers have orders for some products all the time. In these situations, you just take your pieces of machinery, line them up, and run those all the time. With the rest of your equipment, you adjust it as necessary; that's job shop. So for a big portion, you have flow shop. Then for the rest of the products you have a job shop.

Example: Rockwell Space Systems Division makes the space shuttles. Even though they have a half-million parts, each time they make a new shuttle, it's different. The problem is that you can't make anything repetitive or add any value to that operation. But some processes are repetitive, like the plating department. No matter what different parts come through, it will undergo chroming, cleaning, or some other treatment. The only thing that varies is the part that comes in. So we improved their process, because it didn't make any difference what each part looked like—it was all going get the same treatment anyway.

Combined Work Cells

Figure 9-4

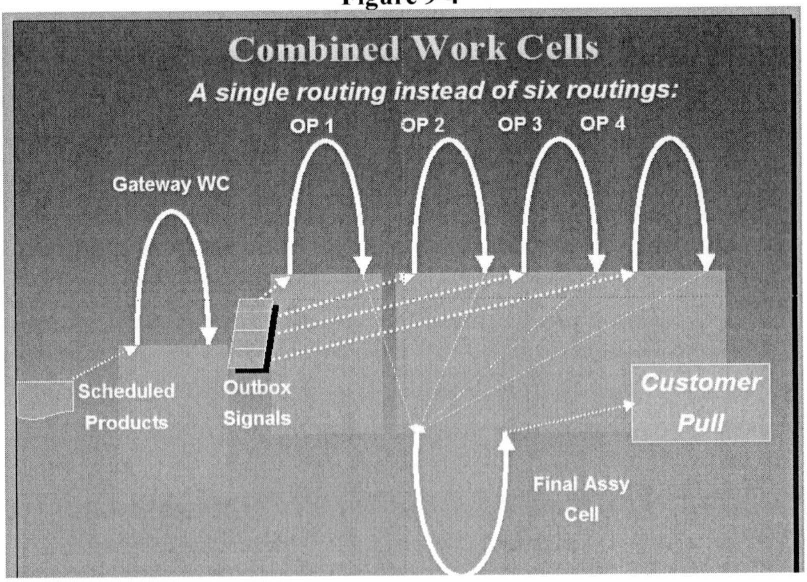

Figure 9-4 shows combined work cells. We looked at a single cell before. Now we're looking at a group of cells working together. Maybe the product being manufactured has some assembly to it--a fabrication process, such as something needing to be welded, glued, or data entered, etc. Each of these half circles is a work cell. They come in through the first one, called the gateway work center. Inside, there is a process that will be performed. In some companies, a saw cuts things. In other companies, they have a data entry place or a complaint department. From there, the item may go to any one of those next operations in the diagram, showing an outbox with four slots and four operations. Each one of those operations is completed, depending upon which unit needs one next. Then the input people put it in their out box. When the rest of the cells need something, they take the item and begin their process. Next, when they're finished, they locate whichever one is ready for them to take and process. They complete it and pass it on in turn. In the case in Figure 9-4, they have a final assembly cell, so that it all goes there. This bottom final assembly cell then goes to what the customer pull is.

Lean Speed and Inventory Reduction

This is one of the most important points of this course. When you reduce the lot quantities, you are increasing the speed. If you have ten units that come in for processing today, and they have to go through ten operations, then, by the time you finish the day, you may only have one unit coming out the other end. But if you have one come in, and you pass through ten operations, it will go out today. If you have another one coming in right behind it, it will go out today. The smaller lots take less space, less handling, less movement, less cost, and less carrying cost than with larger lots or batches. Speed is increased every time you cut the lot in half, because the material passes through twice as fast.

- Speed of throughput quickens as WIP (work in progress) is reduced
- WIP falls in proportion to lot size reduction
- Inventory and time are the same thing
- Safety stock is smaller when lots are reduced
- Problems stand out more visibly

Lot Size Impacts

A lot is defined as a quantity of product produced together and sharing the same production costs and resultant specifications.

Figure 9-5

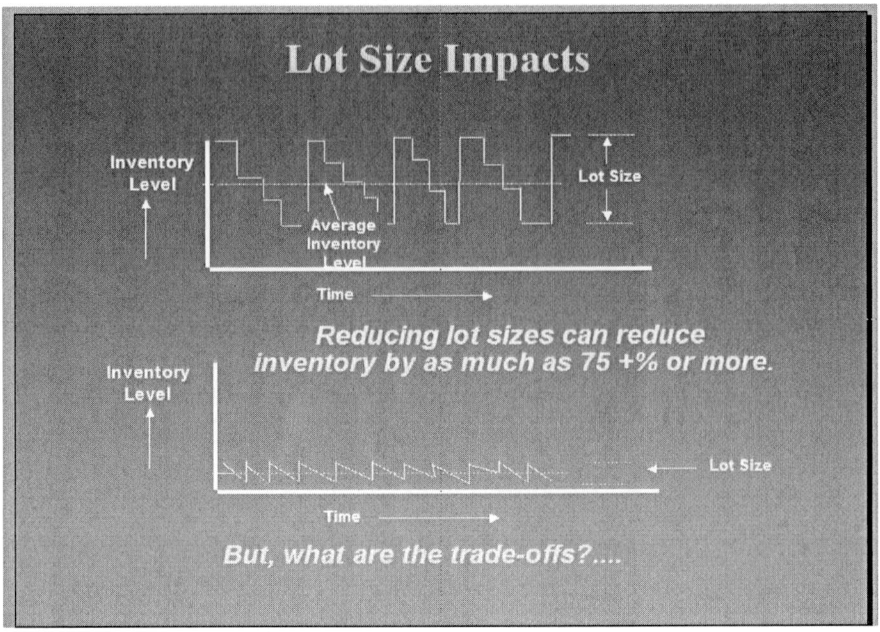

Figure 9-5 shows the impact of lot size. If you look at the first amount where there's a large quantity passing through, the average inventory is half the lot size of anything here. At the bottom, it shows how, if we have very small lot sizes, the amount of inventory is much lower.

Demand, Supply, Lead Time and Inventory

Figure 9-6

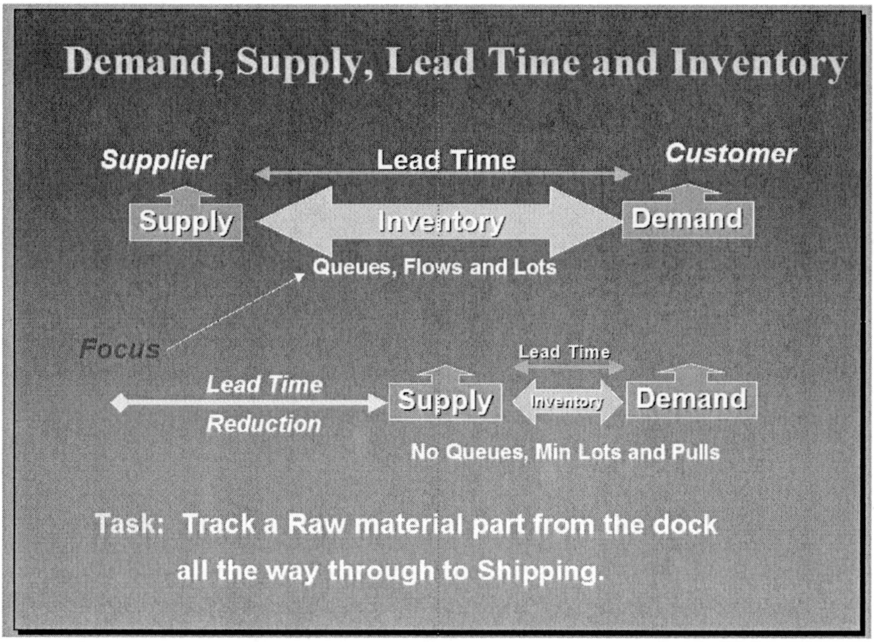

Figure 9-6 is a graphic example showing that the larger amount of inventory—or of things that you need for the processes of your business--the longer for it all to go through. If you have a supplier that brings in the inventory on the left-hand side, it goes through to the customer at the other end. As it passes through, it stays in queues, flows, or lot quantities. Because there is a large amount of it, it takes a long time for it all to go through. The customer finally gets it at the other end, after a long period of time. If, however, by reducing those lot quantities, the lead-time is reduced, the whole flow through from supply to demand is cut in half, just by cutting the lot sizes in half.

Many times people load up their warehouses with finished product to sell to customers. That's another lead-time error: parts that you're paying for just sit in your company until they're gone. The idea in lean is that customers pull it when they need it, and then you just move it forward when they pull it. So, one moves, the next one moves up behind it, then the following one moves, and the subsequent one moves up behind it. And this movement can either pertain to the work orders or the actual represented part.

Just-In-Time Systems

The concept of Just-In-Time (JIT) means to have only the right quality part in the right place at the right time. The JIT pull system is essentially the heartbeat for the flow in the business of lean manufacturing, lean operations, or lean production systems, etc. This pull system is actually a signaling system that allows you to have only the right quality part in the right place at the right time.

Here the word "only" means that you're going to use one; if it's not a quality part, it isn't even one, because you can't use it. This means that you must have a coincident quality program that allows you to have quality product to pass through. Let's say that somebody is doing some work in distribution and that they have orders to ship today. If we have a person working there who doesn't always get them right, we may go out and pick the order, but once we get all the way to the last stage, and we're ready to ship, the checker may find that it's the wrong material. The waste of manpower, time, lead-time, and customer dissatisfaction, etc., all came from the fact that it wasn't the right quality data in the order to begin with. Often the front end is wrong or will have more errors than anywhere else in the company. This is because it's the most unknown.

JIT Applies To Companies with:

- Controllable work patterns
- Medium to high volume
- Repetitive patterns
- Defects less than 3%
- Assembly operations
- Easy to understand processes
- Predictable patterns

For JIT or lean to greatly improve your processes, your organization needs to have some or all of these characteristics. If you have two or three of these, then JIT is applicable. The more you have, the more applicable using JIT pull systems in your business will be.

Internal Pull Systems

Figure 9-7

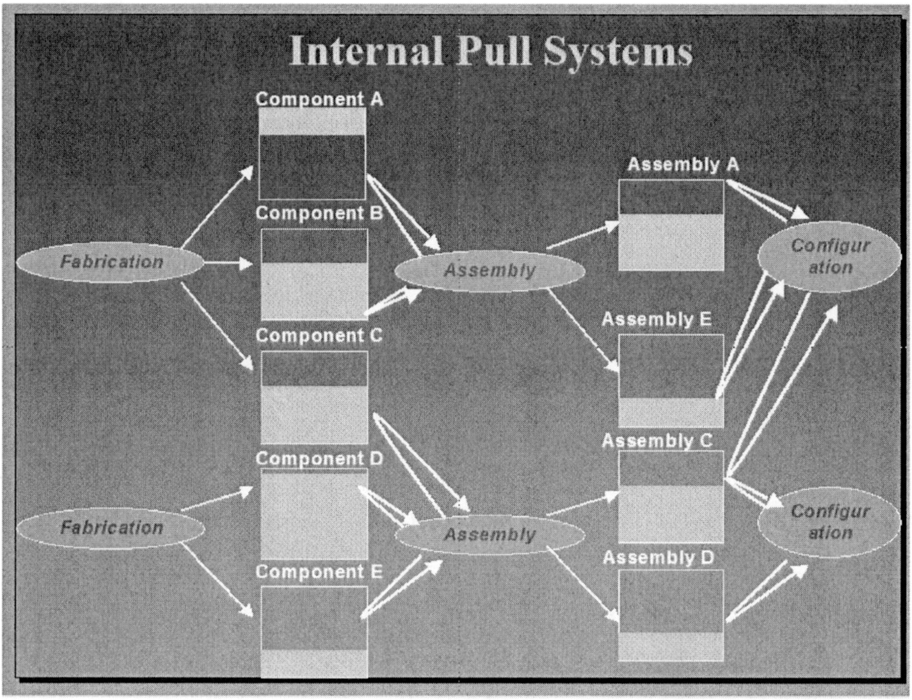

Figure 9-7 shows how easily the internal pull system works. It begins on the right-hand side of the chart, where it says “configuration.” That’s where elements will be brought together and pulled through the system toward their final configuration: assembly, shipment, package, envelope, etc. Each of the assembly areas (A, B, C, & D, etc.), are workplaces, and a customer at the end of the configuration is pulling work through those workplaces farther downstream. When the customer needs something and takes it, a signal goes back to the origin of those components. For instance, in the top right-hand block, there are three arrows going out and back. In Figure 9-7 those are actually circular arrows that tell the system to send a signal from configuration down to assembly (D or E or A), and to have the worker pull one unit. This signal is sometimes called a production card (or Kanban), which just says: “pull me another one or move me another one”. Kanban is another Japanese term. Loosely translated, it means "production card," "billboard," or "sign." This method of signaling in just-in-time production uses standard containers or lot sizes, with a single card attached to each. This facilitates a pull system in which work centers signal with a card that they wish to withdraw parts from earlier operations or suppliers. The term is often used synonymously for the specific scheduling system developed and used by Toyota Corporation in Japan.

Rules For Kanban Cards

1. "You can't work until yours is gone."
2. When material is taken, the Kanban card goes back to the previous station to build the next container quantity.
3. All movement is in standard containers of one part or minimum lot.

Example: I once worked with Price-Pfister, which had a just-in-time line for their Black and Decker Division faucet-manufacturing group. We found that certain assemblies had to be made in order to set up a JIT line. You start with some kind of a pipe, and then the valve goes on it, then the fittings go on it, and then the other things go on it… until it's finally completed and boxed. The process required fourteen stations in this one series of operations. The people were tested, proven, trained, and worked the line, so that, when we started up production, they knew what they were doing. When they started, their first round of boxed output was around 360 units in a day, and it was ready for purchase in local hardware stores. But eventually, as time went on, inventory buildup problems began showing up. Now, there are rules for signals controlling how materials flow through the Kanban line. Let's say that a worker gets ahead of the system in his work. If there's more pull, then he's allowed to put something from his point onto the pull. But if his work hasn't gone, he's not allowed to work on another piece. The rule is that "you can't work until yours is gone." If he ignores the rule, he'll trigger the next one in line, and then materials will start building up.

However, that doesn't slow everything down to the speed of the slowest worker. If I only have, let's say, 14 units in the flow, then I get 14 slots. All I have to do is look at the one that doesn't have one on a post… or one that doesn't have one on the next post. If there's one on a post that hasn't gone, then we have trouble, because, if there is one still sitting here, and there's one with an empty post with somebody working on it, then the employee has obviously broken this airtight rule. So whoever the slowest person is will be the one who's still working while nobody else is. What will happen is that, if the customer takes one unit, it'll begin stripping the line out, so that you'll see an empty post, another empty post, and another empty post, etc. And the unit that this person is slow at working on will still be here, so it immediately highlights the bottleneck. Every effort should then be focused on off-loading the bottleneck.

Lean Visual Methods

- Scheduling is done through signals that are visually obvious, such as:
  - -- Move signals
  - -- Parts status
  - -- Start or stop
  - -- Customer demand
  - -- Supplier delivery

These are examples of lean visual signals. a card to move the unit on, an empty pallet to fill it up and send it back, an empty bin to get it and send it back, or a flag to say, "Come and get one." There could be more than 100 different versions of this, including turning a light on, shutting a light off, yelling, making a telephone call, faxing, etc., inside or outside of the factories or offices. Anything can work if it will give the signal that a unit was just taken, so that the next person can work.

JIT Pull "Cards"

Figure 9-8

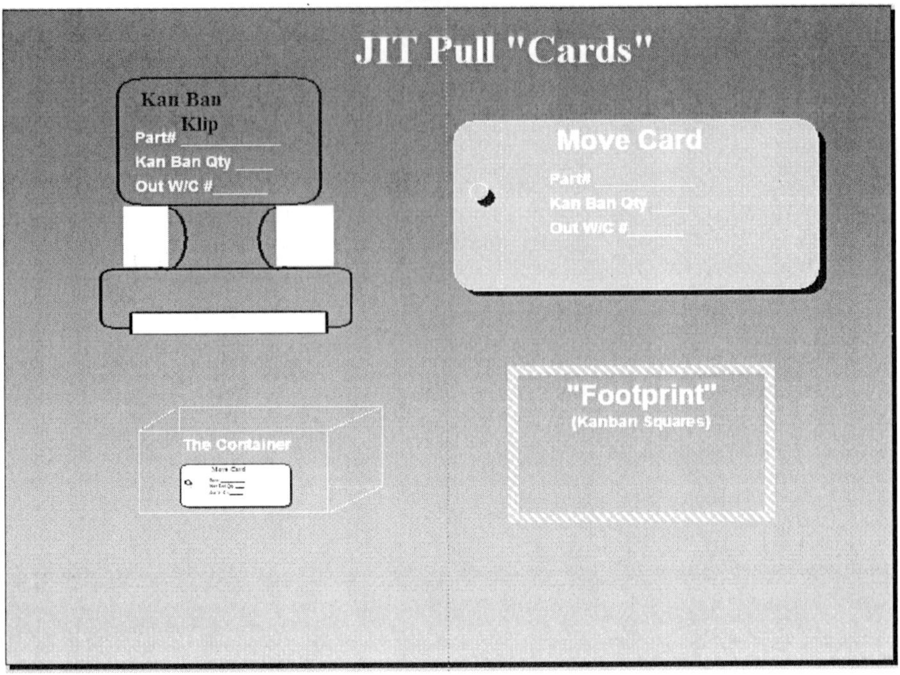

These are samples of pull cards. Each one could take the form of a footprint or marking on the floor, or a marking on a counter top, or on a desk. If that mark is empty, then you can work. If there's something in it, you can't – at least not on that task. You could have a system that uses two boxes. One box could be for a particular flow, while another box would be for a different flow. So, if one box is empty, then you could work to fill the other one. When this one is done and the first one's still full, then you don't work on either until one of them disappears.

Pull System Exercise - 1

Figure 9-9

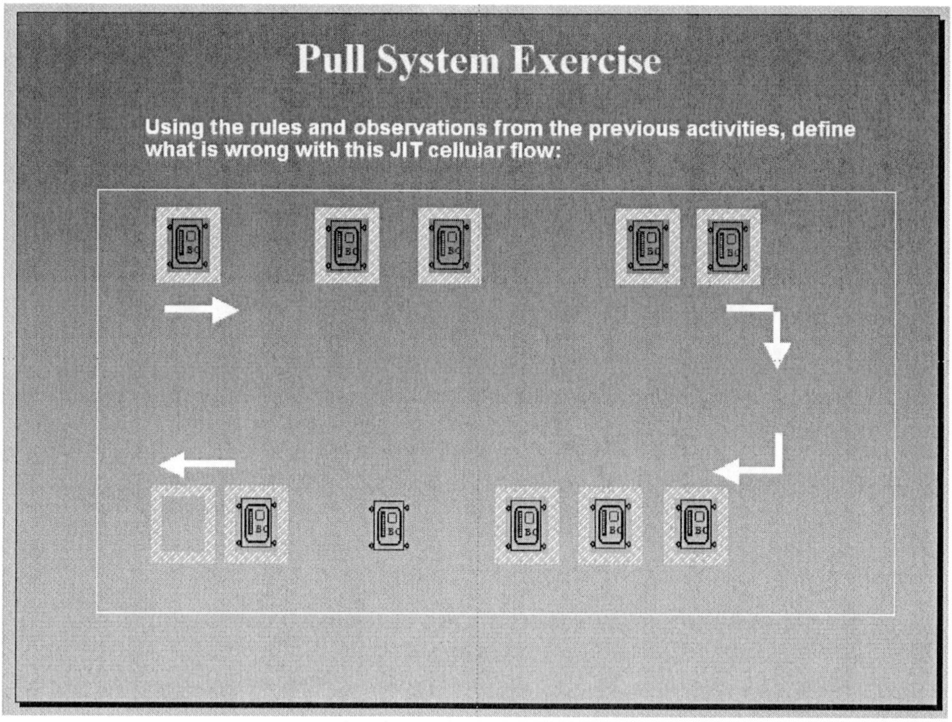

Using the rules and observing previous activities, what is wrong with this JIT cellular flow?

There are two things wrong. One is that, in the bottom center hole, there is a unit sitting without a box around it. That means that the person in the previous box has pushed it out into the open place. They shouldn't be doing any pushing, because it's a pull system. The other thing that's wrong is that the box on the other side of that open space isn't moving, and there's a hole after it. That box simply represents the workplace, work cell, work center, or a marking on the tabletop or on the pallet, etc. Each of those units are like a little cart with parts or a unit being assembled that's moving. The cart, which is the unit we're making, has been pushed out into an area where there is no box. The box is a dedicated place where work is done, and that's the only place at which work can be done. You can't have materials lying around.

Pull System Exercise - 2

Figure 9-10

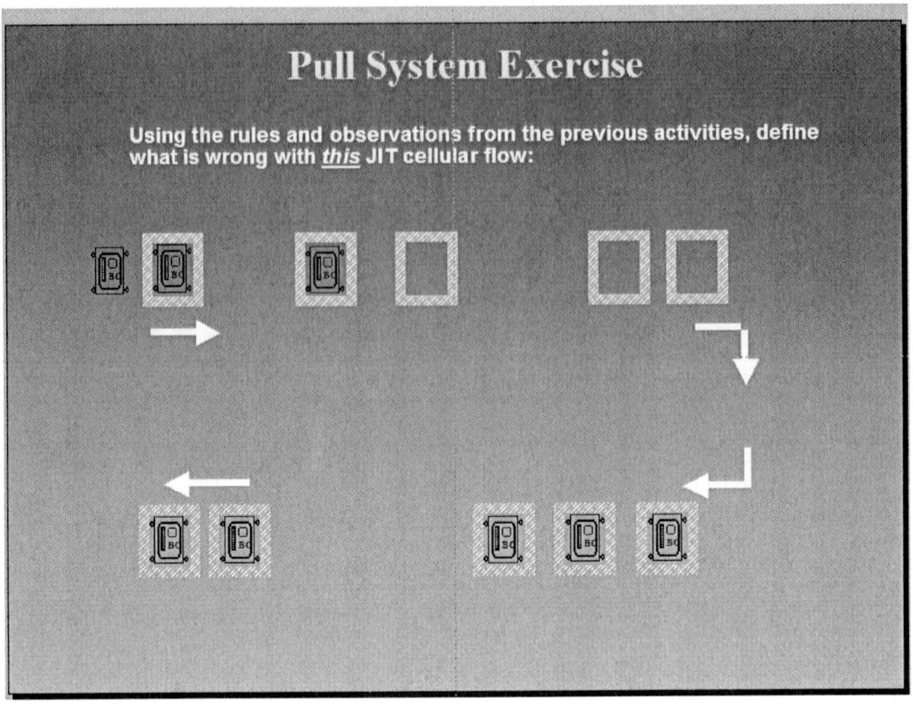

Figure 9-10 shows another exercise. It's the same as the last one, except that the first thing you see at the very top is that the unit got pushed forward. The first one that's sitting outside of the box got pushed from somewhere else. They're just stuffing it into an area where it shouldn't be. Proceeding after the second one in there, you get empty boxes. This tells you that if you see three empty ones, in the next minute you're going to see one more empty one, and then another empty one, and another.... It will just keep on going. That means that the worker at the top is just not getting his or her work done. The second box hasn't moved. Yet downstream, people are all working and doing fine. Therefore, the minute you start seeing empty slots, there's a bottleneck just in front of the slots.

To recap, the two problems are that:

1. There is a bottleneck
2. Somebody outside pushed it

Supplier Process to Process Flow

Figure 9-11

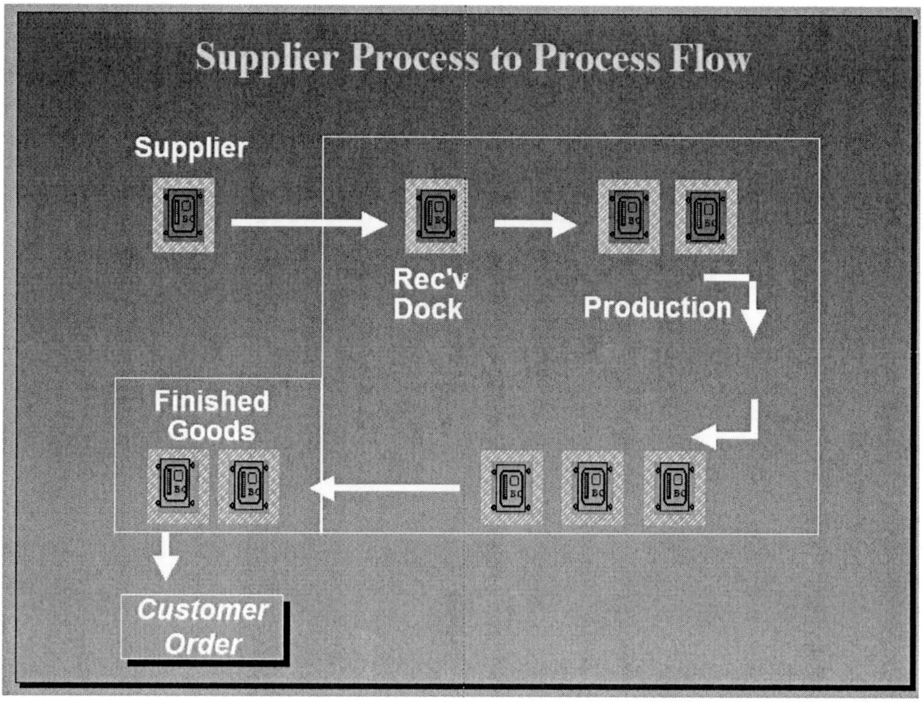

Figure 9-11 is an example of how a company should look. It doesn't have to say production; it could say anything, like typing, word processing, or data entry, etc. The idea is to have a system that is driven by customer demand or customer order. In Figure 9-11, this is the cell that it's pulling through. But each signal is pulling it backward, all the way through the cycle.

Example: The Veteran's Administration (VA) has a leaner system for filling prescriptions than many HMOs. The ability to respond is so much better in the VA than it is in a lot of other places because they do all the work. If you go to an HMO or similar system to get a prescription filled, you have to talk to somebody, or pay a doctor's bill, etc., to get some medication. They may or may not give you a prescription, or they may refer it, and then you have to go somewhere else before you can finally go down to the pharmacy and have it filled. Then you often have to drop it off, and then go back again later to pick up the medication. It's a very cumbersome process. But with the Veterans Administration, there are only a few workers filling about 5,000 prescriptions a day. It's all automated with a machine that can keep track of the integrities of what goes in and what comes out. As long as they make sure to put the right data in, along with the right names, tags, and flows, this bar-coded process is accurate and fast.

Chapter 9 Homework Assignment

Using the flattened bill of material and restructured routing from the exercise in Session 3:
1. Construct a physical layout of the flow through the new router with defined workstations in a cellular formation.
2. Estimate time to pass through the cell and then calculate the cycle times for each station in the cell.
3. See if you can balance each workstation cycle time in the cell to be somewhere near equal.
4. Check throughput time again and compare with the old flow.
5. Compare the distance a product traveled through the previous flow with the distance required to pass through the new lean cell.

Chapter 9 Quiz

1. Muda results from Kanban inventory, but not from rework, counting, or paperwork. True or false?
Answer: False.

2. What layout optimizes custom model designs in its flow?
   A. Process flow
   B. Cellular flow
   C. Product flow
   D. None of the above
Answer: A is correct.

3. What is the basic rule for JIT pull systems signals and movement?
   A. Work as fast as you can
   B. Only work when you have a unit to do
   C. Don't work until the one you've finished is taken away
   D. Keep a few items between you and the next one in line

from you
Answer: C is correct.

4. What does the reduction of lot sizes accomplish? Choose all that apply.
   A. Reduces time through the work cell
   B. Reduced time through the warehouse
   C. Reduces time through production

Answer: A, B, and C are correct.

5. What would be the effect of reducing lot sizes on all parts by 50%?
   A. Inventory turns go up
   B. Inventory goes up
   C. Supplier delivery times go up
   D. Warehouse stock goes up

Answer: A is correct.

6. Which of the following are JIT Pull signals? Choose all that apply.
   A. The heartbeat of the process flow
   B. A replacement for production control and scheduling
   C. Only workable between suppliers and customers

Answer: A, B, and C

Chapter 10: Leaning the Work Itself

Objectives:

- Apply and use machine set-up reduction tools.
- Define and test the elements of the "5S".
- Use the theory of constraints to identify obstacles in the flow.
- Be able to gain visibility, improve flows, reduce space, and shorten lead times through the 5 improvement steps of constraint management.

Setup times are a factor in virtually every process, even if it's simply putting a new e-mail address list in your computer because you want to update some e-mail contacts. First, you have to prepare the list, which means you have to work: you have to call this place, call that person, do this, look that up, go get a book, look up some more things, get some envelopes, etc., if you want to get the lists into your computer. Most of the time, a lot of the work in a process centers upon making preparations or changes to the area in which the process takes place. Here, the goal is to find out how to eliminate, from the workflow, all of the waste involved with setup activities; such as walking, talking, and collecting, etc. An example of this can be seen with the filling of prescriptions mentioned above. When fully computerized and automated, the setting up, repeated authorizations, and physical running around etc., are eliminated.

What 5S Is

Five S means to:

1. Sort
2. Select
3. Scrub
4. Systemize
5. Standardize

Some businesses are run in a cluttered, dirty, and messy environment. Often other firms in those same businesses have immaculate work environments and offices. This indicates a certain sense of business style, because letting clutter remain is not really conducive to the work quality. For example, you don't need to keep catalogs from the 70s and the 80s. All relevant catalogs are online now.

The Theory of Constraints

The Theory of Constraints is no more than bottleneck management. One of the core rules in bottleneck management is that the rate of the bottleneck sets the rate for the entire system, wherever it happens. Often, the person who looks like the bottleneck is not the one who is creating the problem. You need to locate where the cause of that problem is, and this almost always requires that you employ flowcharting techniques to locate it. Let's say that people come to work and that they have a shift change. The problem with a shift change, of course, is that you have to stop something and then you start something. Many things that go on in between, such as greetings, visiting, having a snack, and getting coffee, etc., between the start and the stop of shifts, result in totally wasted time. Companies statistically lose about an hour a day here.

Reducing Set-up Times

The purpose of set-up reduction is to run smaller lots.

- Make them less consequential
- Get the crews excited about reduction
- Focus on bottlenecks first
- Videotape and brainstorm the set-ups
- Move internals to externals
- Co-locate and prep all tooling
- Question the need; suppliers help
- Set continuous improvement targets

Example: I worked with a company called Major Paint & Varnish Company for some time. Some equipment was always breaking down. My role was Assistant Plant Manager and my job was to ensure that, when the work was ready to be done, I'd get it out, get it set up, get it expedited, and get it back. When somebody would come back to the shop, they'd bring back the work order they'd worked on, we'd talk about it for a while, and then I'd look around, find a job, and see if that was good for them. Then I'd fill out the sheets for it, give them some materials, and then let them go take care of that job. That's about a 4.5-hour process. Over time, I did research and found that the biggest waste of time in certain jobs is travel time. People walk around too much, both doing the work and being sociable. So I would project what items were needed for whatever type of job they had to do—let's say it was to repair a valve, patch a roof, put in some electrical wiring, fix a switch, or whatever. I'd make sure they had their tools and all the necessary parts. I established a rack of elements, in sequence, for the jobs they were supposed to do, and these materials were always there. For those that had to work in other locations, the parts were set up for them to take as a kit to the work location. I would track and report their time to the head of the company, and it soon became very productive.

Find out what you can do in your workplaces to position things so they're where they need to be. As mentioned earlier, one company placed its printer in a location that caused the workers to walk 725 miles year in order to do the print jobs. With that wasted time, you could buy a brand new printer and put one at every desk, if you had to. Some companies have come to realize this, others haven't. The latter are usually firms that think they're saving money, but don't realize that it's insidiously seeping away by people walking around and doing things.

Example. I once worked to help a famous company that makes door knobs and door levers. They had machines that took 16 hours to change over from one kind of a knob to another. But then they would run the machines for days and weeks before they'd do another changeover. It took 16 hours, but the fact is that it was possible to cut the setup time in half by taking the waste out of it. This would allow them to now run two customers' products instead of one, which would serve other needs they had. This situation wasn't about failing to save time, but really about making more products available in the same time. The change we made in the management of setups and changeovers was to automate it, so we could make sure that, if a machine needed to be running, it was always running. We did that by co-loading the parts, co-locating the parts, and making sure the teardowns and setups were all standardized.

One rule fundamental to this is that setups and changeovers are done only where machines or operations or people are running—or working back to back. The work flow bottleneck, wherever that may be, is the one where you do setup reduction first. You can make it a setup reduction program, and expand out to make all others faster, but it must always be done with the bottleneck first, because it runs, shuts down, changes over, and runs again. That's the secret in reducing setup times.

Set-Up Time Objectives

- The ideal is zero time, zero cost, auto set-up
- Less than 10 minutes (SMED)
- Practice for perfection
- Reduce variance
- Goal: To reduce set-up by 50% on any set-up selected

It would be optimal if we didn't have to change anything and we could keep the operation running, like a dark factory. This kind of manufacturing location gets its name from the fact there are no people working there because there are no lights.

Example: Many watch manufacturers, such as Citizen, make their products in dark factories where everything is automated. The machines automatically place parts, change them, and make adjustments. When the next unit comes, the machinery automatically adjusts itself—all computer controlled—and the next brand of watch or model gets made. You go in there to check it once in a while, and automatic lights come on. Other than that, when you leave, the lights go off. That's saves electricity too, despite the fact that it's been fully automated. It's sometimes possible to get a 50% reduction of setup time without ever touching the physical thing.

The Purpose of Set-Up Reduction is to Run Smaller Lots

- Not to produce more product
- Not to reduce set-up cost

SMED: "Single Minute Exchange of Die" = Less than 10 minutes
Single minute exchange of die (SMED) is the concept of setup times of less than 10 minutes, developed by Shigeo Shingo in 1970 at Toyota.

Set-Up Reduction

Setup time is the time from the last good part, event, form, sheet, page, or art, etc. to the next good one. The objective, of course, is to reduce that time to a shorter and shorter period. This not only reduces your overall throughput time through whatever business you're in, but also increases your ability to pass it through faster. This happens as you run smaller lot quantities, which take less space and less time.

Internals to Externals Definition

Figure 10-1

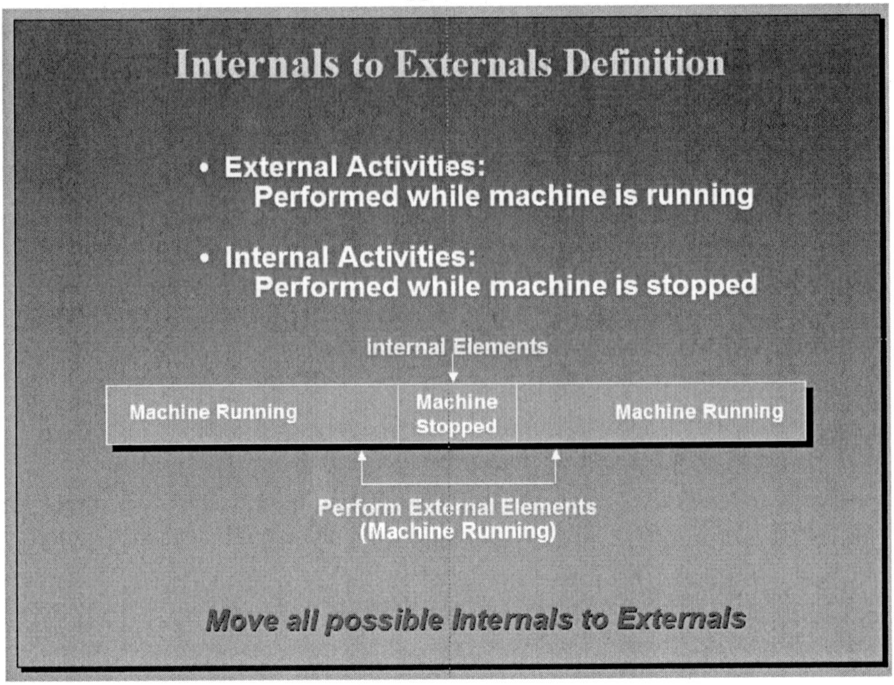

The ultimate secret for the setup reduction issue can be referred to as internals to externals. If you're doing an operation on a punching machine, in order to change whatever is in that machine, you would have to either reach in to take it out, or go to the copier or printer and change heads or the paper, etc. But during actual work operating times, you can't put your hand in the machine without getting it lopped off, printed on, spilled on, or burnt. If you have to put your hand in it and you didn't stop the machine or the operation, then you have to at least have it down for that time, so that you can actually put your hand in it. So anything else, like preparing the next materials to be coming, preparing the next paper to be printed, preparing the next work order to be done, or preparing the quality check that has to be done, etc., has to wait until they shut the machine down. Only then can they go off to find this, get that, move this, talk to somebody there, or take a break, etc. This is what internals are.

Externals, as shown in Figure 10-1, are things that can be done while the machine is running; either before the machine shuts down or after it starts back up. This can include cleaning, sweeping, or putting stuff away, etc. And that machine is down only when it absolutely has to be down.

Everything else can be done before or after. That will almost invariably give you 50% savings in setup time, without even touching the machine yet. Then you can still look at additional changes to make with the machine for more improvements.

Reducing Lot Sizes

Figure 10-2

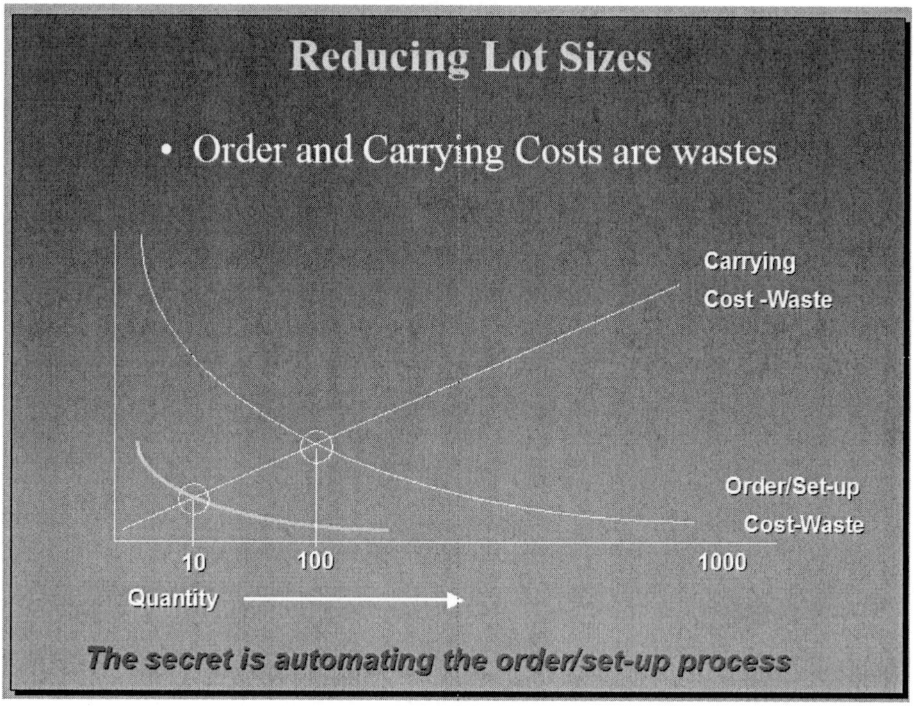

The graph in figure 10-2 shows how there are two costs for every time an order is placed. The placement of the order comes from a salesperson calling in, an internal operative approaching you with the next new item, a maintenance operation getting a work order, or an art shop getting a request to build or to make something, etc. Whenever there's a new order, there are at least two things that always happen with it. One of them is the carrying cost, which can be about 25% of the price paid for any item you have to buy. The other cost is the order cost, which is the cost to place the order. The case illustrated in Figure 10-2 shows a situation where, if you want to place an order, say, for some print paper or some other samples that you need for sales, you can't just print it because you want to. You can only do so if you get a signal from a computer system or an authorized manager who told you to replenish this item. When it comes in, somebody has to receive it, count it, check it, post it, mark it, pack it, unpack it, count it, check it, etc. Then, some computer data entry has to be done while it waits, and next, it finally moves off into a location where it might be put back in the paper stock area. When it finally gets there, it will sit here for a couple of days before it actually gets put in stock. Then you put it in stock, transact it, and you tell the world that you have some more to offer them. It could be 2 - 20 days, which could be a long time.

The trick here is that, if there was a way that you could order things without spending all the time and money for purchasing, ordering people, warehouse people, receiving people, handling, material handlers, forklifts, and electrical power, etc., then there would be absolutely no cost for the replenishment. So, you ask the questions, "Why am I going through all of that? Why can't I just have somebody else do that? Is possible that I could have the paper company take care of ordering my paper?" They've got the biggest vested interest in it and they have to come out anyway to bring it and check it out. They can even have their driver come by and check it out if you request that, and then you don't have to fool with that paper anymore. This means that it could go through its entire cycle, and your cost to order that inventory is now very small; usually 10, 15, or maybe 20% of the cost you had with the old system. Now it's all taken care of by the supplier, and the only time you pay for it is when you use some. It's already here and they already brought it, but you can set it up so that it is consigned inventory in your company. The paper can be given to you and then, next week, when they come in, they look at how much you've used, and then they can bill you. That way you don't even have it on your books, since your money is not tied up in it.

So if you can reduce the lot size, the way to optimize the ordering cost is to automate it, outsource it, have it done online with a computer system so you don't have to do it, or set it up so that the supplier's salesperson comes through and checks every so often, doing it for you.

Figure 10-2 displays how, if you have reduced your cost to order inventory, then you can order smaller amounts of it, and you don't have to buy large lots anymore. If you buy once a year, you'll have a lot of inventory all year long, but you'll only pay one ordering cost. The idea would be to only order it once. You can set up a contract for the whole year, have the supplier come in, take care of it, fill it out, and then invoice you once a month. It goes straight to payables and you don't have to deal with it, except to check it every 3 or 6 months. The majority of today's businesses have gone into having suppliers intimately involved with the processes of materials movement working inside of their companies. They trust that the suppliers are not going to try to just bring in stuff to sell off because it's on consignment, and the company doesn't have to pay unless they use it.

Example: A company that was supposed to have some big bolts was running out of them. So I asked around: "Who's supplying this?" They told me who it was, and we called them up to find out why there were some empty bins here. You can't have empty bins in a lean system. We found out that it was a new driver, a new truck, and a new follow-up guy. He didn't know what to do with certain kinds of things. So they made a change, which didn't involve us. When you look at the illustration in Figure 10-2, the order quantity that you may be buying could be reduced to half or a quarter of the original order quantity, because your ordering cost is greatly reduced by automating the ordering process. That's what this picture really means. It's a major secret used in lean operations. It's also a major piece of an entire inventory management course

Variable Cycle Times in a Flow

Figure 10-3

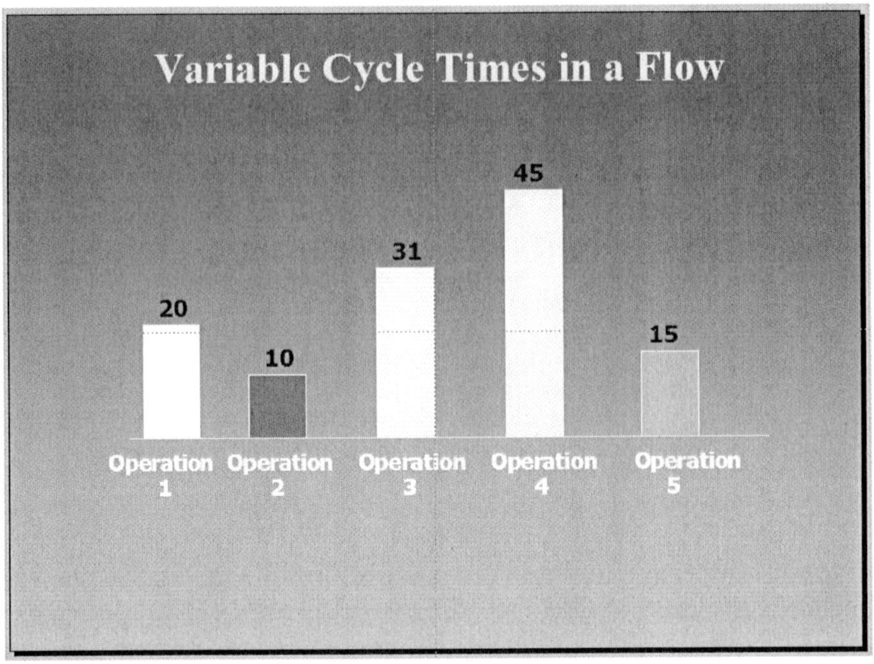

Figure 10-3 is a quick chart which shows the variable cycle times in a flow. Let's say that you've got five things lined up and they're all doing their work. Some take 15 minutes, some 45, some 31, some 10, and some take 20 minutes to do the work. Those that are in the low points, like the 10 and the 15 may appear to be not working or not productive, because they're sitting around. So we may have more work for them.

Effects of "Keeping People Busy"

Figure 10-4

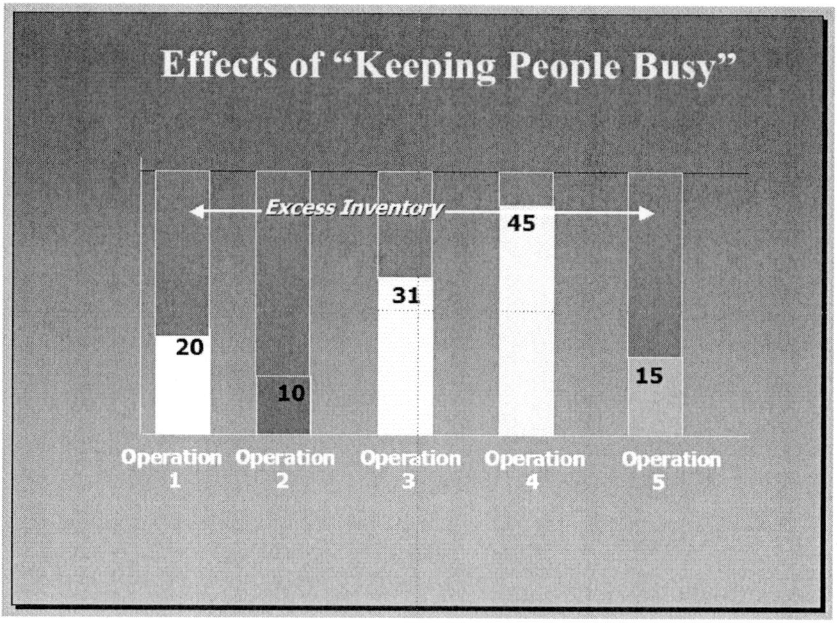

Figure 10-4 shows how keeping idle workers busy doing other kinds of work that may not be necessary more or less creates excess inventory. It's better to cross-train people, so that they can work in any one of the processes. That way, if you're short in a particular area, or fall behind a little bit, then you can shift your workers to where their efforts will be productive. This cross-training is a big rule in lean operations, no matter what the work is. It could be typing, order entry, computer data, or any other tasks. We want to make sure the workers are always working on those things that are tied to the major flow.

Preventive/Productive Maintenance

- Uptime is productive time
- Unplanned downtime is waste
- Operators should "own" their machines
- Shift company focus to maintenance
- Treat PM the same way you do setup time reduction.
- Remember, PM adds value!

Pull systems require working equipment. Therefore, doing preventive maintenance is adding value, because your uptime on machinery is greater. Making operators "own" their machines allows you to avoid having to do maintenance or repairs on the equipment at all. Ownership is a major element in good business practices because, if equipment operators feel that they have ownership, they will have more pride in their workmanship and they won't let others tamper with or inappropriately use their machine. They will also be much more attentive to the needs of the equipment.

Constraint Management

Definition:

- The synchronization of all resources in timely concert with market demands.
- All activities must be tied to the rate of the slowest constraint within the overall system.

In essence, constraint management means managing the bottlenecks. Goal: Every effort must then be directed at the constraining resource to improve the throughput.

Follow your customers' needs. If the customer's needs slow down, then you should slow down accordingly. The same applies for the cases where the customer speeds up. The idea is to get rid of the buffers that insulate customers from producers so that, when the demand moves, the supply moves very cleanly, right along with it. That's the trick: to make it so that there's no time or inventory between the customer demand and your supply for it. In constraint management theory, the bottleneck sets the rate for the whole system. That means, all activities must be tied to the slowest constraint in the system—where the bottleneck is. It doesn't help to improve a non-bottleneck work center in isolation. So the bottleneck must receive focus as the center of managing constraint for everything. To increase throughput, we simply bring down the bottleneck.

Constraint Management Objectives

Figure 10-5

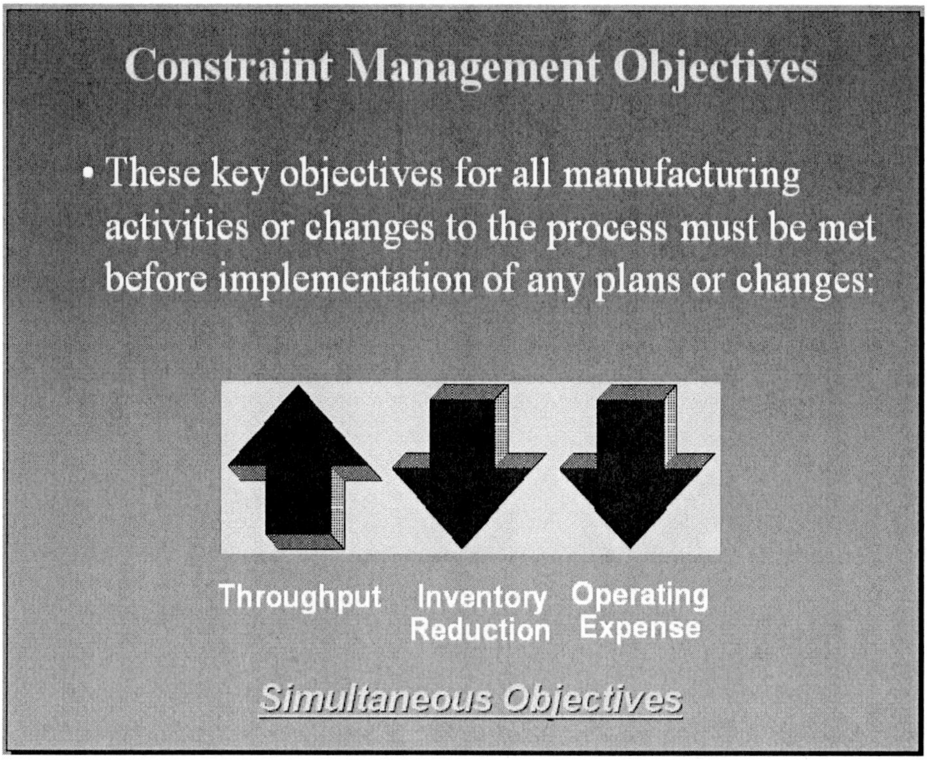

If you use the tool in Figure 10-5, you would be correct every time.

Everybody does a cost reduction program. That's really good, but a cost reduction program is only the third arrow. In reality, all three arrows exist simultaneously.

TIOE Definitions

This comes from a book called "The Goal" by Eliyahu M. Goldrat. In this case, throughput is the rate at which the system generates money. You may think that throughput is passing something through the system. But when the work of the process makes money, that's when it becomes real.

- Throughput = The rate at which the system generates money through sales.
- Inventory = All the money the system invests in things the system intends to sell.
- Operating Expense = All the money the system spends in turning

inventory into throughput.

Throughput means throughput to sales, not throughput to inventory or throughput to the warehouse or throughput to a customer's warehouse where you don't get paid for it. Inventory is just the money you spend to get materials. Operating expense is the money that the system spends to turn inventory into throughput.

Scenario: I'm the manager, and you come into my office to tell me that our main computer in the reproduction room went down. I'm now going to ask you some questions about the situation.

1. What is your solution?

Your answer will probably be that we can't get a machine, so we just need to send everything out.

2. Will your solution increase throughput through our system here?

You may respond that when we get the machine back after repairs that it will produce more; and hence will increase our throughput.

3. Will the inventory be reduced?

You may answer that the inventory we had before wasn't running because the machine went down. So, if we take that inventory and move it outside somewhere, it might come down, but we're going have to get it back in again, and then we'll be able to move it through our system here. But, if we have to go outside and buy the completed product and we still have our inventory here, then the inventory is going to go up. That's the opposite direction we want for the inventory arrow, which is supposed to go down.

4. Will the operating expense go down if you go outside to have these things purchased?

You may answer yes. But, if we're now going to use an outside source—which wasn't a factor in our Figure 10-5 box calculations, it's an additional part of the box. So then, that additional part is higher operating expense, which wasn't there before. The point is that, if you can meet all three arrows on any solution provided, then you will be right every time. That's the trick.

"The Goal"

- What is the goal of a business?
- What are the three key objectives?
- What are the five steps to improvement?
- What is the Real Goal?

The goal of a business is to make money. If it's a non-profit organization, then the goal should be to improve the process, although it often isn't. That's why it's sometimes very difficult to implement lean with people in governmental organizations and organizations where people volunteer.

The Five Steps for Process Improvement

We have just been going through what Goldrat calls a process of ongoing improvement. That doesn't mean improvement or continuous improvement. The difference is with the words "process of improvement." When any problem occurs, you can't simply apply a solution just because it worked before at another place or with a similar problem. This time it may not be relevant. There are improvement programs, such as TQM, sigma programs, and others, that don't really add throughput value. They often sound nice and look like they show the bottom line, but they may result in having more physical inventory in finished stock. This is not what we want, although they can certainly improve some areas, such as having happier workers or less work-in-process inventory.

The lean process involves:
1. Identify the constraint
2. Exploit the constraint
3. Subordinate all to the constraint
4. Elevate the constraint
5. Go back to step 1

Exploiting the constraint means that you try to get as much out of the process as you can while the constraint exists. Then you subordinate it, or make sure that that no one will be putting more work on the constraint. That's the trick. Next, you elevate the constraint, which means to unload it. So, if the copier breaks down, as in our copier example earlier, we simply off-load its work onto some other machines. When the broken machine is repaired, then you're back to normal.

Example: This printing bottleneck will set the rate for the entire day for all of the processes. This is because every product we make has to have a book with it, and we've lost our ability to make books effectively right now. If we send items out without a book, it's not a complete product, no matter how good the product is. It can't go without the book, and the copier facilitates the book. It's really very easy. Once you've done that, your constraint has virtually gone away. Then, we go back to step 1.

So there are only three steps. The constraint pops up and you find it. Make sure it's the big one for the day, week, or month. Then, once you identify the constraint, you simply take whatever time it takes to get it off-loaded.

Example: Let's examine a case with the company that made doorknobs. There was a machine called the clicker. Part of most round doorknobs have a little latch in them that locks the door. But a hole has to be punched out with this little machine, and it would punch hour after hour, going click, click, click.... There was a problem when it wasn't running properly throughout the workday with the other processes. The issue was that it had to run, not 24 hours a day, but during all working hours. The productive time had to be a full 16 hours every day in order to barely make the output for the entire factory. If that clicker wasn't running, the output from the factory was down, money was down, income was down, and people were laid off. So we determined that this part of the process was a constraint that should be off-loaded, by using the clicker and having it running at times like during breaks, through lunch, and after, etc., to make sure there was always enough work to keep the main things going after these second operations were done. But I'd come in often and find that this clicker wasn't running. So I'd go to the production manager and ask her why. She would go to that area and chastise whoever was working there to get it up and running again—and to keep it going. Yet, sure enough, I'd go in a couple of days later and find that the clicker wasn't running again. I'd have to fight this battle repeatedly. So much was dependent on one little machine, so it was astounding that they weren't constantly watching it.

Overcoming Process Problems

- Identify the process constraint (problem): "What inhibits flow through this area?"
- List all inhibitors
- Sort the list by TIOE
- Pick from the top of the list

To list all inhibitors, you ask where the constraint is. In drawing producers, it could be a blueprint place or an outside supplier. For some workplaces, the constraint is in having a lot of safety measures and too many meetings. Another company may have people who say that the floors are too hard and their feet hurt. It could be that you have purchasing shortages, or that half of your crew of six are new people. Write that down. That's what brainstorming is. This gives you a list of what your inhibitors are to getting the work through your area. The people who are most knowledgeable about the work being done in an area are the ones working there now. They are the ones who need to look at this and do the brainstorming. It's not done by a bunch of brains out there, somewhere, that don't know this work anyway. It's in the workplace or, as the Japanese call it, the Gemba. And all the things around the Gemba (workplace) as a composite are called the Gimbutsu – the working tools, things, and activities, etc.

To sort the list by TIOE, you think: throughput, inventory, and operating expense. Sort the list by which ones of these give you the most throughput, inventory reduction, and cost or operating expense reduction. The steering groups or managers can now take the list generated at the work levels in all areas and put those together. They can re-sort the list and they'll find that there are several documented problems in different areas. There may be several purchasing problems in different areas, some bigger than others. Now the entire company is working on just the top two, three, or four constraints to the entire organization. Maybe the steering committee gets the list back and it highlights the fact that the number one item really is documentation. The number two item could be purchasing. The number three item is maintenance. The number four item could be the paint department, and so on. These are now listed from highest to lowest importance for the entire company, and they're all tied directly to the flow through the company.

Process Flow Diagrams

Figure 10-6

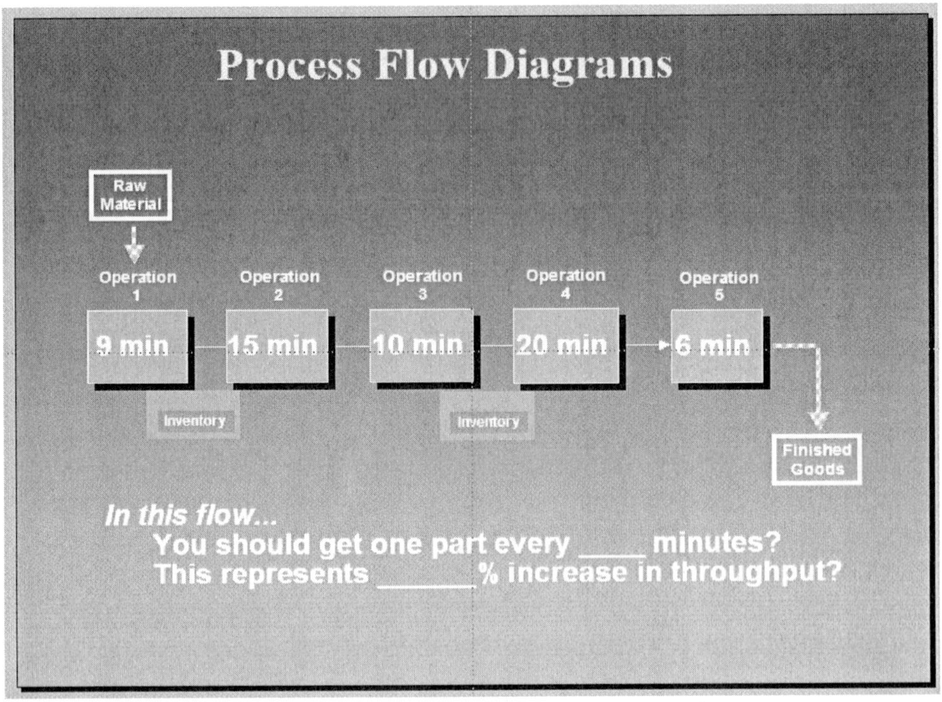

Figure 10-6 shows one very clear picture of the top four or five items to focus on over the next period of time. You give the list back to all the workers, and they begin doing improvement activities on these problems. That's where overcoming process problems ends. The whole company is all working on the top few. If they don't have one that's on that list, then they work on one that is further down on the list, because it's not in their area, or it's okay for them. That way, everybody in the whole company is focusing on accomplishing tasks that clean up these processes for the next several months. And then you go back through and you reiterate this once every six months or every year to check if there are any new problems that need to be worked on. It's a marvelous system, and it's elegantly simple.

Chapter 10 Homework Assignment

1. At your plant or any flow of work, identify at least 5 operations in a sequence and flowchart them like Figure 10-5 (the last diagram in this chapter).
2. Record the cycle time for each operation and identify the bottleneck operation in the flow.

3. Calculate the increase in throughput if the bottleneck time were reduced.
4. What percent increase did you find?
5. What actions could be taken to reduce the bottleneck?
6. How far down should the bottleneck be taken?

Chapter 10 Quiz

1. What is the purpose of set-up reduction?
   A. To increase production in the same period
   B. To run smaller lots
   C. To increase speed through the factory
   D. To reduce cost of doing set-ups

Answer: B is correct.

2. What is meant by "internals to externals"?
   A. Move excess product away from the processes
   B. Have all manpower ready to start the set-up as soon as the machine goes down
   C. The last good part to the first good part
   D. Move every action possible out of down period on the machine

Answer: D is correct.

3. Automating the set-ups is the secret to lot size reduction. True or false?
Answer: True

4. TPM is Total Production Maintenance. True or false?
Answer: False. Total Preventive Maintenance is the correct answer.

5. Which of the following is NOT one of the three key objectives for Constraint Management?
   A. Increase throughput through to sales
   B. Inventory goes down
   C. Supplier delivery times go up
   D. Operating expense goes down

Answer: C is correct.

6. What will the 5 step process for continuous improvement do? Choose

all that apply.

A. Meet the goal of every manager
B. Eliminate non-bottleneck inhibitors
C. Save time where ever applied
D. Focus efforts on the what truly needs to ship

Answer: A is correct.

SEGMENT II:

Lean Support Systems and Functions

Chapter 11: Leaning the Support Functions

Learning Objectives: Clarify the role of Purchasing and supplier interfaces.

- Restructure incoming and outgoing movements for lean flows
- List ways to lean the inventories and actions in warehouse and distribution facilities
- Define agreements with suppliers
- Define the best materials movement techniques

Inventory is in support as well as in line, because these items are part of the product movement. But purchasing is not, although it brings in the materials that go into the flow. Purchasing is integral to the flow, but it's also off to the side with respect to problems such as resolving inventory shortages. Engineering is the same way; it's off to the side, but necessary before anything can flow through. Lab is similar; it has to be done in certain sequences of doing specific things and, although they are a support function, they are also a direct line function, because they are sitting in the flow of the information. It's a rule that the flow of information is the flow of materials or work and is the flow of money in a business. Like an eternal mirror, when you look back and forth, it just keeps on going. All the other functions are either in line with it or in support of it off to the sides. This includes accounting, payroll, and quality departments, as well as sales entry and credit departments. But at many companies, the focus is less on the main goal of making money, and too much on the support functions. And much too often, this focus results in creating inhibitors to the flow of work and the making of money.

Example: New designs of forms and other records data management can create cumbersome new systems and unnecessary bureaucracies. It's important to structure the support functions in ways that don't add inhibitors to the system. They should only assist with passing the flow through, so that we don't have any loss, waste, cost or time in the system.

The Supplier/Customer Process

Figure 11-1

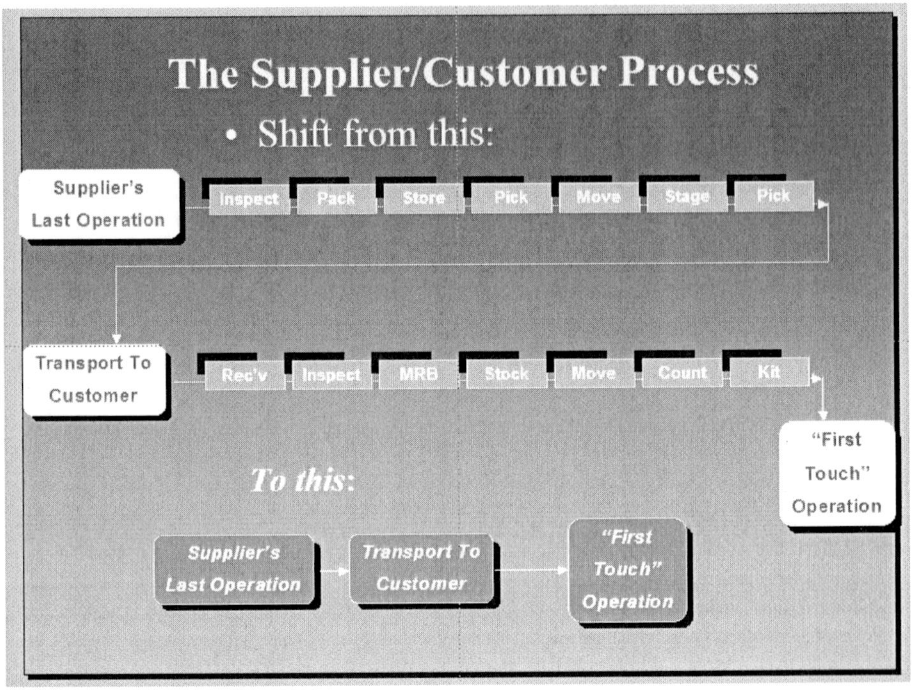

Figure 11-1 shows a common situation. In its last operation, a supplier in the top left box (for example) wraps the item in tissue. Then they took this item and they inspected it, checked it, packed it, stored it, picked it out of the stores, and then moved it into a location where it is staged to ship. Then it's transported to the customer in the left box on the second row. Now, on our company's time, it comes in through receiving, inspection, and material review board, which checks the quality for any problems. Next it gets moved to stock, and then moved to whoever is going to use it. That person will then count it, check it, and then put its parts together into a kit. Finally, the first operation or the first touch for us is going to be when somebody here in our operation picks it up to use it, sticks it in a printer, on a wall, or maybe installs it in a machine. There are about 15 movements or activities here. Now, the boxes on the third (bottom) row show how things should be. The last operation at the supplier is the one where they put it in a box and also ship right from where it was. They put it in the shipping box, rather than in another kind of box. It goes directly through transport, the middle box, and then it goes directly to the user. It doesn't go through receiving, inspection, checking, testing, counting, validating, or any of those previous stages. It simply goes directly to whoever's going to use it. So it comes in right through the door, right down the hall and into the user person's office, operating place, or machine. This eliminates all of the extra steps of the previous system, which didn't add value.

The Supplier/Customer Interface

Figure 11-2

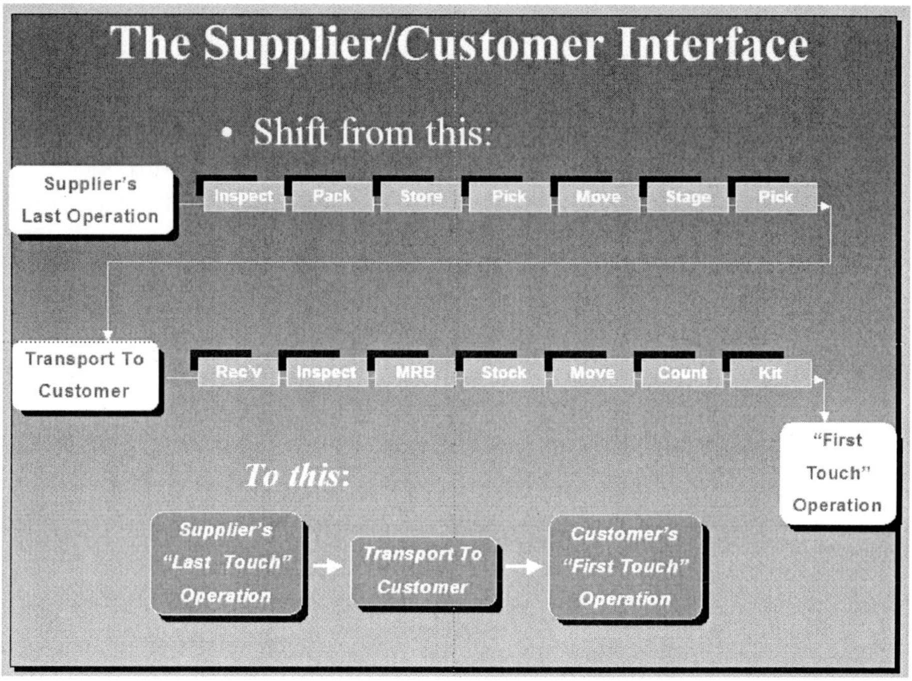

Figure 11-2 shows an optimum example. You want to have suppliers that are close, and few in number to supply the many different products you may have. You need them to be at the very best, proven high quality levels, highly responsive to needs and changes, and able to work well with pull signals.

Key Supplier Attributes for Lean

- Distance
- Fewer in number
- Highest quality levels
- Rapid response to needs
- Works with pull signals

Lean Material Supply

Minimizing paperwork and transactions with suppliers:

- Use the grocery industry as a model
- Gathering movement information
- Supplier replenishment triggered by use
- Users can manage movement and replenishment

Agreement with Lean Suppliers

A simple annual agreement can be broken down into smaller pieces, based on your forecasted demands. From there, the supplier doesn't ship until you signal.

- Three points to the agreements, longevity, small lot quantity, and don't ship "till I signal"
- Quantities pegged to production rates over a horizon - MRP/JIT tools
- Plan for variability of
  - -- Schedules
  - -- Pricing
  - -- Specification changes
  - -- Technology
- Set lots as small as possible based on demand

Relationship Agreements

- Quality
- Lead-time
- Packaging

- Labeling issues
- Signal mechanisms
- Cycle time
- Measurements

Inbound Transportation

Alternative methods for inbound freight

- Daily or timely Milk runs
- Shuttles
- Combination sweeps
- Outsource carriers
- Freight consolidators
- Consolidation points

Example: I was working with a company in Minneapolis that made railroad lights and flashers. The light body is a large, enclosed, zinc cast. The purchasing person told me that they were getting the smallest incoming received lot quantity that they could get. He said, "We are now ordering 400 at a time, and that's the lowest amount we can get." But I saw that 400 tended to last for quite some time in the areas that we were trying to clean up and cut waste. These things were in wire bins that took up a lot of space. We couldn't organize the flow, so I went with them out to the factory, without asking for the salesperson. We let them know we were coming and we just set up a tour with the plant manager. As we walked through, we asked him to show us the stuff they were doing for us. We saw these casting things all lined up and how they processed them. Next we asked them if they ever ran less than the 400 they were running for us. They said that it happens, depending on what they were doing. So I asked him if they could run 200 or 300 for us, and he said that they could do it with no problem. We were talking to the production guy who did the scheduling and who could make that decision. It allowed us to get the smaller number and to change our supply agreement.

A milk run is where several suppliers in a certain geographic proximity to a company's location can use their trucks, cars, or mail system to stop and drop, and stop and drop... all the way around the cycle every day. You eliminate a lot of the cost of having to buy larger lots and take space in warehouses, etc. Also, a lot of the waste of handling and time disappears.

There are also ways you can bring it in from far parts of the country by doing freight consolidation. You can set up Chicago, and then all deliveries for all suppliers in Chicago go to one location. Then it's cross-docked onto a single truck, which comes in with multiple small quantities. Yet it's a full truckload, maximizing your freight savings by having multiple small lots, instead of a lot of small deliveries made all over the place. There are lots of freight handling companies, freight forwarders, or freight consultants that do just that kind of work; they help you optimize freight.

A combination sweep is just taking one group at a time and bringing it in from a consolidator. Or the transporter makes two or three rounds on one day and then different ones on other days. This is basically a scheduling issue, so that you or an outside freight company is doing all the pickups and deliveries for you in a cycle. It could be your own company, or it could be contract carriers. And then there is the common carrier, which is regulated by the Interstate Commerce Commission (ICC), which sets the rates and fees. If you have trucks for other things you do, then you might do well to have your own system.

Consolidation points means where several suppliers that you may have in different locations, all ship to one drop location, such as Chicago. Then the cross-docked truck fleet, such as Viking, would then pick it up and deliver one load to you. So, you have one truck with multiple small lots instead of multiple trucks with large lots. This is another trick you can use to reduce your inventory.

Streamlining Deliveries from Lean Suppliers

- Specialized vehicles, dock methods timings and handling practices sped up or eliminated
- Methods to simplify packaging, containers, point of origin and transportation paperwork are enhanced for speed

Interface Coordinators

Figure 11-3

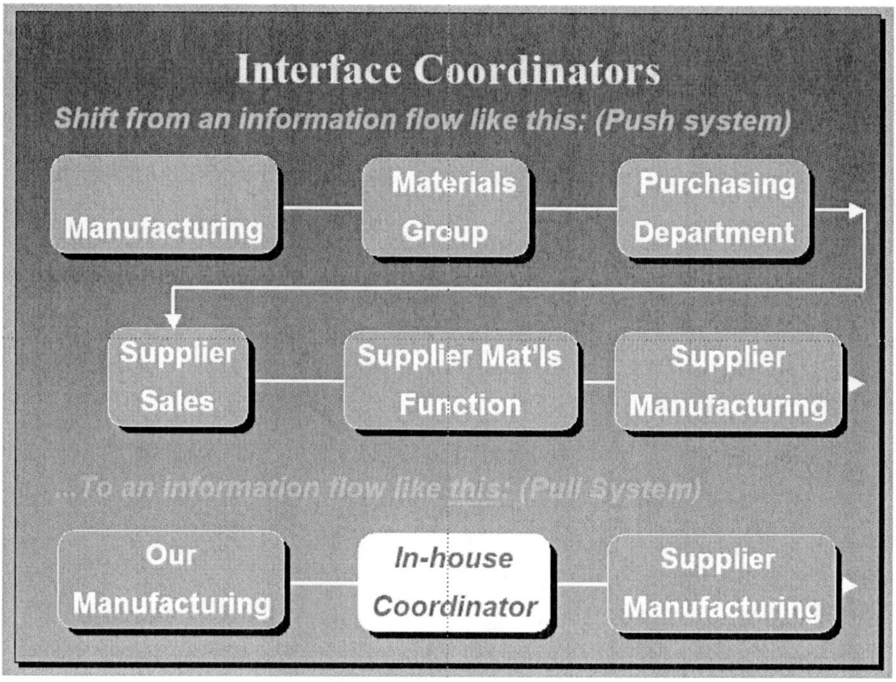

Eliminating Muda from Supplier Networks

Figure 11-4

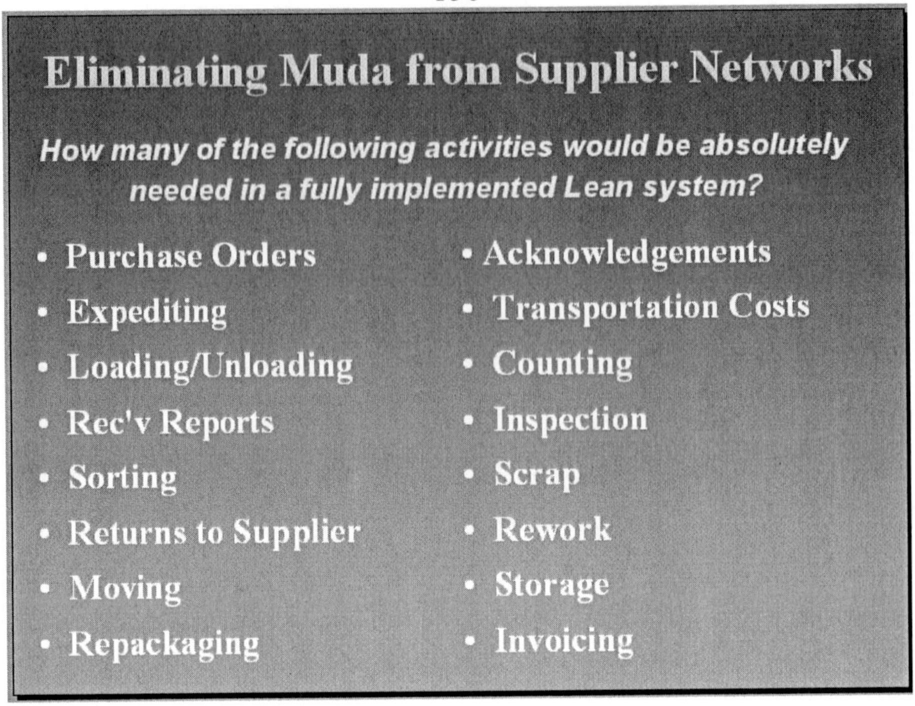

Figure 11-4 shows questions that are a pop quiz for leaning your operations. Let's say that you're able to implement just-in-time pull systems with your suppliers, whether outsourced or contracted from outside to come in and do it. How many of these activities would be absolutely needed in a fully implemented lean system? You wouldn't need purchase orders (POs), because you've got contracts that go on forever. POs are simply a tracking tool. You may need a number, but it doesn't have to be a PO number; it could just be a number for each time you get a delivery, e.g., 01, 02, etc. You don't need expediting, which means you call them up and find out where they are. If you use the just-in-time system, you don't have to call them up, because they're getting signaled, and they've already built it ahead of your need, instead of calling them up when they're trying to make it for your need. It's a very common thing that companies do today. They wait until they need it before they order it. They may set the contracts, but they have to write POs for a product each time they need it, and that's wasteful. Loading and unloading wouldn't be necessary, because the supplier does that. The supplier could also handle receiving reports, either automatically or with bar code, as they drop items off. The same goes for sorting, since everything comes in configured the way you're going to use it inside your company, defined by the supplier for you. There are no returns to supplier, if we have the quality we're supposed to have. And because the supplier drops items right at the user, there is no moving. You have the supplier do any repackaging, since it's cheaper for them to do it than for you. Sending out acknowledgements after you place a purchase order isn't needed, since you don't even have the POs. You're just making releases off the long-term agreement, so there's not even a legal requirement.

There will always be some transportation costs, since somebody has to pay freight to get it here or for you to get it to your customer. It can be included in the price, but the may price go up or get absorbed. Counting, inspection, scrap, rework, and storage would not be needed. Invoicing would all be done automatically on line; whenever you have an item that's completed and you ship it, you've paid the suppliers in the bill of material for those items for the parts that just got shipped. So you accumulate that into a single, automatic weekly or monthly payment. They don't even need to invoice you for those amounts since they already know that they were delivered. Some companies have difficulty changing in this area, because they are paranoid about other people tampering with their invoicing paperwork. But lots of other companies have implemented this automatic system to their advantage, such as the General Motors-Suzuki operation that makes the Chevy Tracker and the Geo Metro.

Chapter 11 Homework Assignment

Schedule an interview with a knowledgeable purchasing agent or manager in your company.

1. Ask them what strategies they may be planning to:
    - Reduce suppliers
    - Reduce inventory
    - Reduce pricing
    - Use supplier managed inventory systems
    - Develop pull systems with the key volume suppliers
    - Consolidate incoming freight
2. Record the answers. Does it sound like a lean plan?

Chapter 11 Quiz

1. What is a key rule to eliminate all wasteful interfaces between supplier and customer? Choose all that apply.

A. Ship to stock
B. Quality Certification
C. Last touch-first touch
D. First touch-last touch

Answer: C is correct.

2. Key supplier attributes for lean DO NOT include highest quality, close location, or the fact that the supplier works with JIT. True or false?
Answer: False. All of these are key supplier attributes for lean.

3. Which of the following are lean Interfaces with suppliers? (Choose all that apply).

A. Supplier Managed Replenishment Systems
B. Purchasing not ordering replacement materials
C. Elimination of receiving inspection

Answer: A, B, and C are correct.

4. Supplier agreements should define how signals are to be used. True or false?
Answer: True.

5. Inbound traffic CANNOT be manipulated to handle small lot deliveries via milk runs and freight consolidation points? True or false?
Answer: False. Milk runs and freight consolidation points can be used to manipulate inbound traffic to handle small lot deliveries.

6. Which of the following will be eliminated by using lean interfaces with suppliers?

A. All Receiving
B. Accounts Payable
C. Material Issues to users
D. Picking Tickets to the warehouse

Answer: C is correct.

Chapter 12: Leaning the Business Processes

Learning Objectives

- Define how people can reduce waste in their management practices.
- Develop ways to sensitize Administration and Finance to lean principles.
- Review and set goals to use lean techniques at work

Deep Hierarchical Structures

Figure 12-1

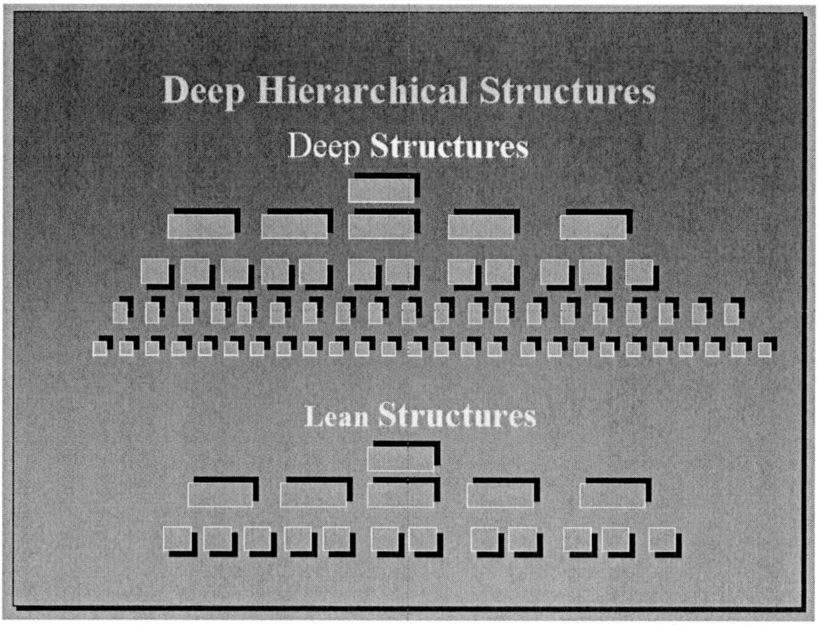

Role Changes for Management

FIGURE 12-1 is a picture of the hierarchal structure of the typical business today. It flows down from the president, vice presidents, directors, managers, and sublevel managers as they solve problems. If you need a problem solved, you have to go from one level of that structure, maybe up two or three, and possibly even to the very top level to get an answer to come down to change the behavior in the problematic location. In the lean structures, although the top may be about the same, much of the lower levels are working in teams or coordinated groups with fewer levels in the hierarchy. This allows you to take away the insulating buffers between different levels in a hierarchy.

So, even in the same company, with the same people, you could have a much less complex structure.

- Planning vs. operating
- No command and control
- Pushing decision making downward
- Team focus vs. autocrat

Example: I worked with a company called Ricoh, which is a printer company out of Japan. Every one of their workers wears one of two smocks. One is beige and the other is blue. Either you're a process operator (blue smock) or you're a support group (brown smock). They didn't distinguish according to titles. They simply made sure that the work was tied to the process and not the person.

A very big failure for companies trying to implement lean is that many company managers can't deal with giving up their authority. They were in charge before, and now, we're letting decision making go to the next level down. The question is, is this a bottleneck or not? If it's a bottleneck, then we'll work on it. If it's the biggest bottleneck, a lot of us will work on it. So, it takes away much of the decision making necessary in the middle levels. With lean, that whole middle level can disappear. That's what the chart in Figure 12-1 is about.

Changes to Pay and Rewards

- Incentive is team based
- Job definitions broader
- Modest base pay levels
- Bonuses tied to company and team performance
- Gain-sharing
- Profit sharing
- Certifications for skill levels

Management Issues for Lean

- Employee involvement programs
- Showing trust in subordinates
- Effective delegation of authority
- Autonomous decision-making at the team and individual levels

- Keep the focus on the goal

Education of the Masses

A continuous and formal training program is in place for lean:

- New employee indoctrination
- Skills development
- Cross training
- Lean manufacturing principles
- JIT concepts for all employees

The goal here is to give the masses models, examples, classes, schools, trials, online instruction, and testing, etc., to help them understand the real impact of what personally affects the worker, laborer, office manger, or administration person, etc. This is much better that some sort of motivation program that gives you a trip to Disneyland or something similar.

Example: I worked with a company in the San Fernando Valley area of Los Angeles. They had a suggestion program in which anybody who had one would be given a snake flashlight—the kind you can twist around. But after everybody got the flashlight, the program died. They would only put a suggestion in the box so that they would get the flashlight. It was an interesting approach, but it did nothing toward actual process improvement.

Managerial Changes

- Middle managers and supervisors will be reduced or re-organized
- Problem solving groups or teams solve quality and process problems—not management
- All employees are part of the problem resolution teams - no exceptions
- Management exhibits consistent support for process or quality problems generated by the teams

The Role of Finance in Lean

- Changes from Lean actions

-- Fiscal reporting to investors looses focus
-- Time and speed is recognized as the key cost and/or profit driver

- Shifting from departmental to process focus

-- It's the processes, not the departments that make the money

Administration Waste

- Batching of paperwork
- Multiple or redundant checks
- Signature cycles
- Meetings
- Walking around
- Multi-tasking

Lean Accounting

- All areas have waste
- Automate accounts payable
- Work closely with purchasing to integrate with suppliers
- Use the computer, not paper to process accounts. Keep digital back-up.
- Structure monthly statement payment

Key Measures and the Bottom Line

Figure 12-2

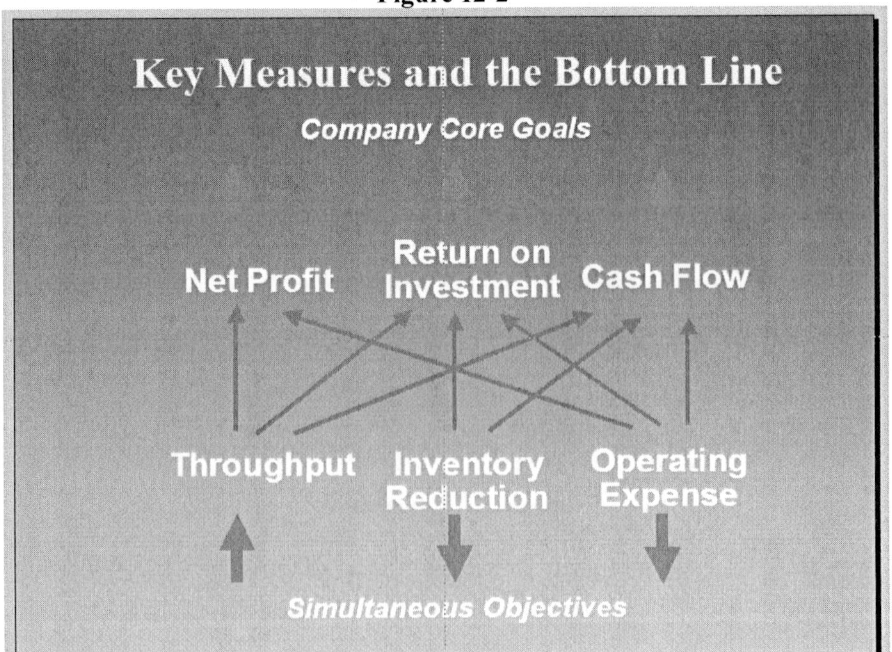

Figure 12-2 shows the e three core measures that indicate to a company that they're doing a good job: increased throughput, reduced inventory, and reduced operating expense. These, in turn, will increase net profit, return on investment, and cash flow—the overall bottom line.

Carrying Cost Impact

Figure 12-3

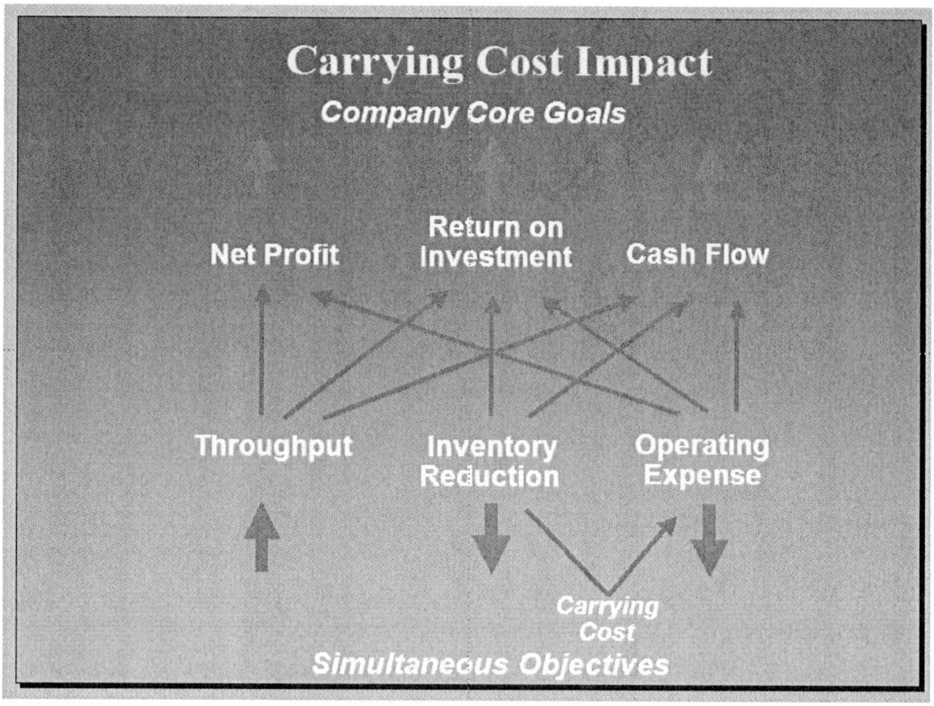

Figure 12-3 shows how reducing inventory reduces carrying cost and, hence, operating expense.

Chapter 12 Homework Assignment

1. Obtain and list the key goals you have in your company.
2. Compare how they fit with the goals we have discussed in this course.
3. Check the competitive advantage goals developed in Session One.
4. What goals should your company be pursuing?
5. Are the Lean techniques described in this course capable of enhancing

your company goals?
6. Show data or calculations to justify your answer.

Chapter 12 Quiz

1. What is the key difference between deep organization structures and lean structures? (Check all that apply)
A. There are too many people in the deep structures
B. There are too many people in the lean structures
C. Decision-making is driven from the bottom in deep structures
D. Decision-making is driven from the bottom in lean structures
Answer: D is correct.

2. Which of the following should pay and rewards be structured to accommodate?
A. Incentive par for the performing individuals
B. Bonuses and/or recognition to the teams
C. Pay for suggestions selected by management as the best ideas
D. Higher base pay levels
Answer: B is correct.

3. Which of the following is a way that management needs to change the traditional way in which it has managed?
A. Promote and support employee involvement programs
B. Be ready to make the decisions when teams need them
C. Run their workers' team meetings in an efficient manner
D. Make sure to check and evaluate the details of every plan they create
Answer: A is correct.

4. The role of finance and accounting has now shifted focus from fiscal reporting to time drivers. True or false?
Answer: True.

5. Which of the following are the most important goals of a typical company? (Choose all that apply.)
A. Net Profit
B. Return on Investment

C. Increased cash flow
Answer: A, B, and C are correct.

6. Increasing throughput is NOT one of the three most important objectives for a company. True or false?
Answer: False.

Chapter 13: Lean Measurements

So far in this course, we have defined lean, shown how it works, and discussed some tools that can help identify and calculate how to build improvement programs. Now we're going to discuss some of the tricks and tools we could use to show the improvement. The use of measurements is the best way to motivate workers towards continuous improvement goals.

Learning Objectives

- Define a lean measurement system that guarantees continuous leaning.
- Define and test the key measures for your company.
- Apply the Three T's methodology to business metrics.
- Chart the level of performance improvement within your company.
- Build a lean measure board.

What are Measures for?

- Point
- Guide
- Motivate
- Report

When the Goal is to Meet Standards

Figure 13-1

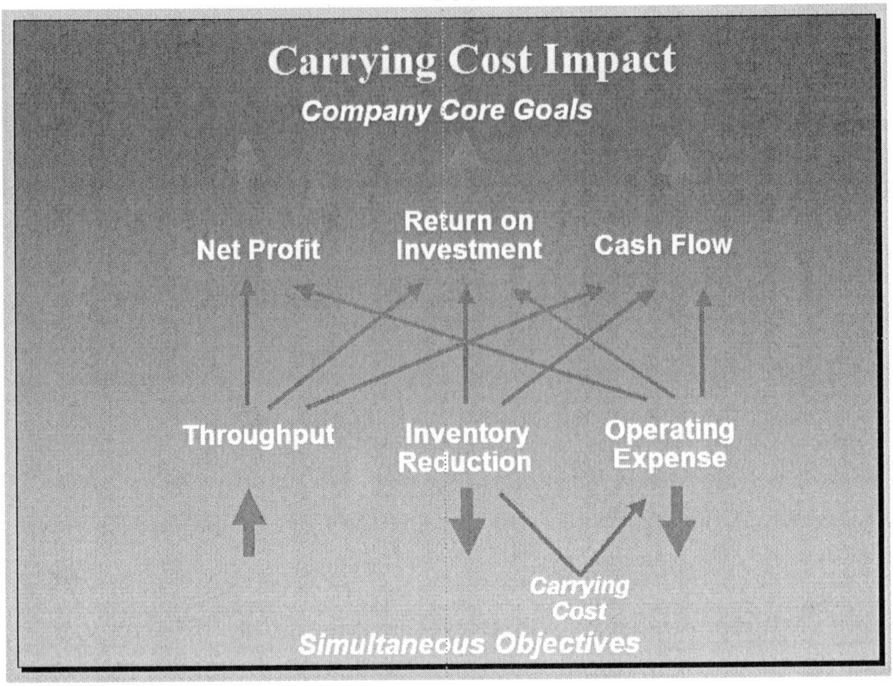

Measure that Count
Figure 13-2

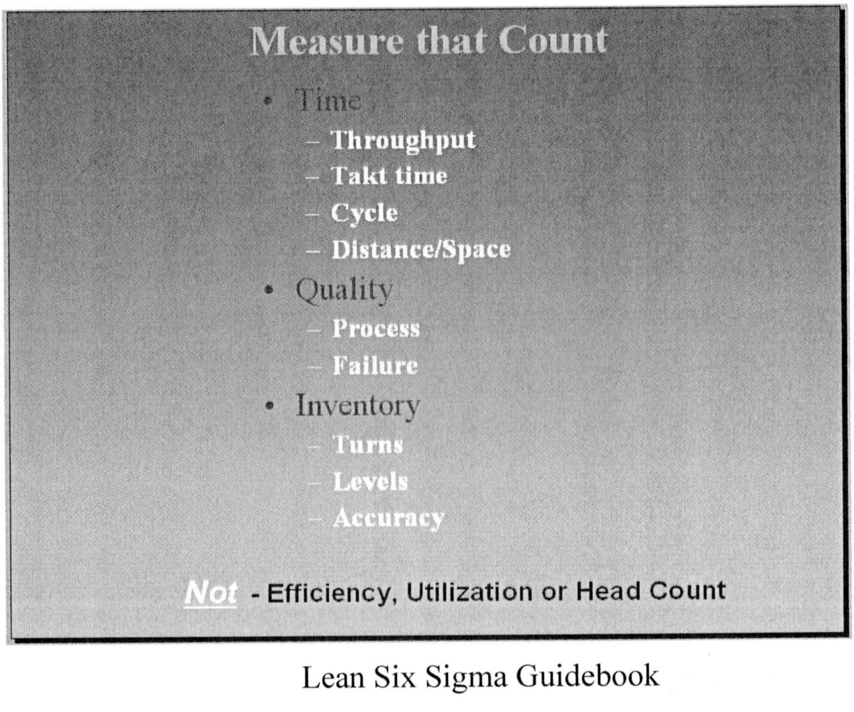

The top section of Figure 13-2 breaks down aspects of time measurements. The first is throughput time, which we have discussed. The second time aspect is called tact time, which is sometimes spelled takt. Basically, it means a typical amount time it takes for a demanded product to flow through a process. Let's say that a product has to go through various departments, such as painting, labeling, and marking, etc. In this example, if you make 60 units per day, which takes 360 minutes in the day to pass it through, then the tact time is 6 minutes (360÷6). This means that no item should take more than 6 minutes in any step through that process, because, if it does, the whole thing wouldn't pass through in 360 minutes. That's what the tact time is.

Cycle time is simply the time it takes to do one specific thing in an area. Often confused with tact time, cycle time is simply the period from the last piece to the next piece. For instance, you've just finished a piece and then, just a little bit later, you just finish another one. It's the time to cycle through one unit of anything. You also measure quality and failure, then you measure inventory, if inventory is an issue in your company. In lean, you don't care about measuring efficiency, utilization, or head count.

What to Measure – The Global Issues

Figure 13-3

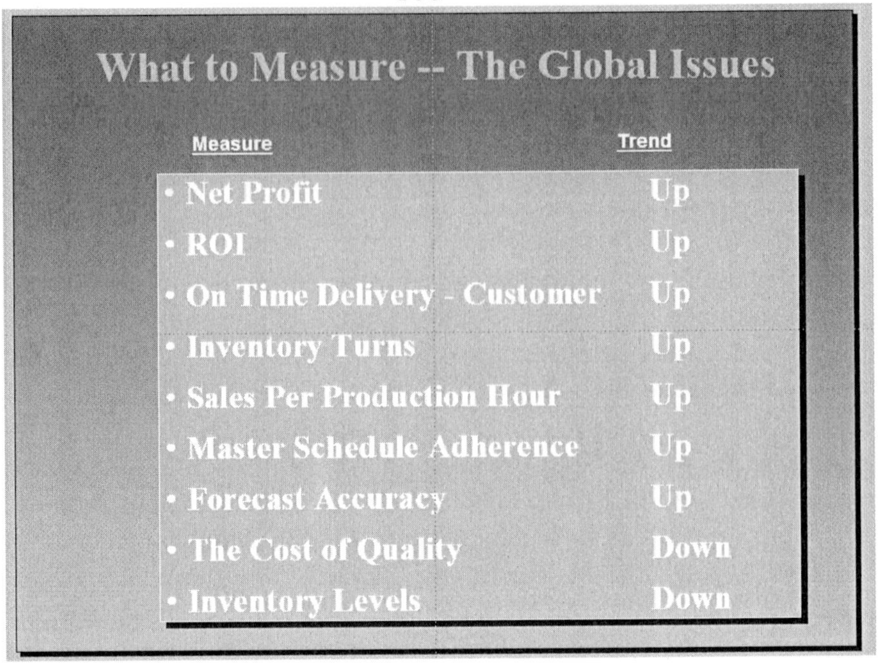

In Figure 13-3, there are various things that may be good for you to measure in your company. Notice that there are no numbers or percentages, because what we'd like to see is a constantly improving set of measures. So every one of these has either an up or a down; there are no break-evens or flats.

What to Measure – The Local Issues-1

Figure 13-4

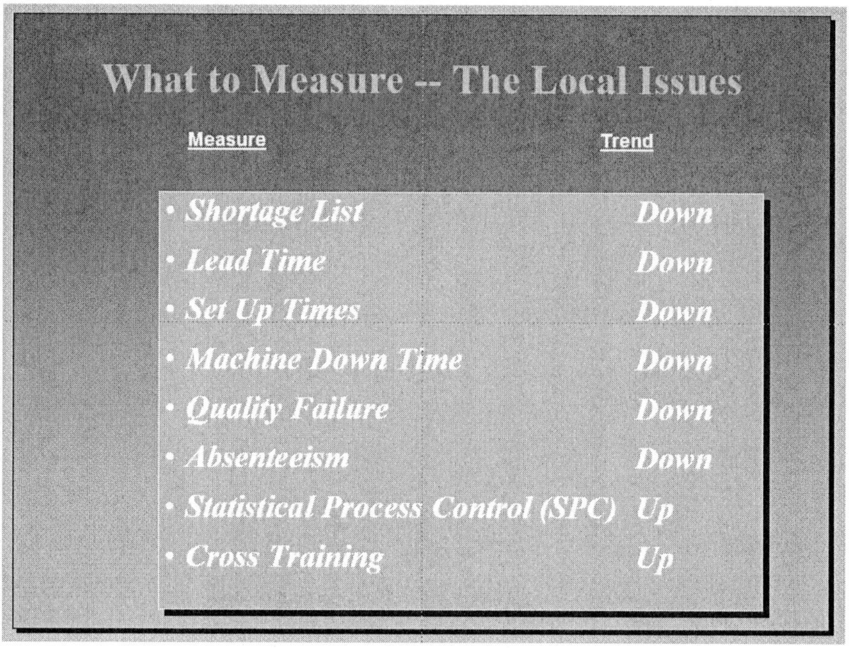

In Figure 13-4, these local measures are closer to the operations of people and their work.

What to Measure – The Local Issues-2

Figure 13-5

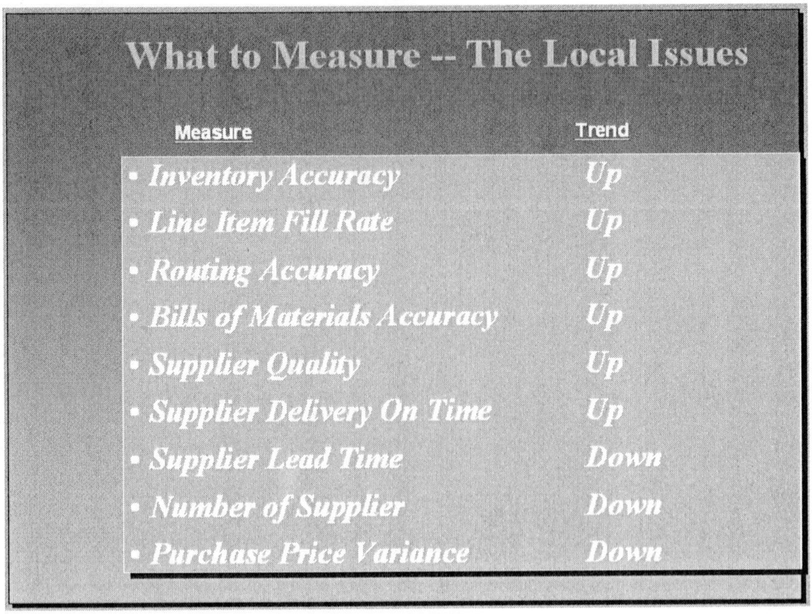

Figure 13-5 shows the increases and decreases (ups and downs) as detail levels that might relate to your business. You can pick other numbers and put them in here, because there are lots of things to be measured. But they should be all directed at the T, the I and the OE (throughput, inventory, and operating expense costs).

Figure 13-6

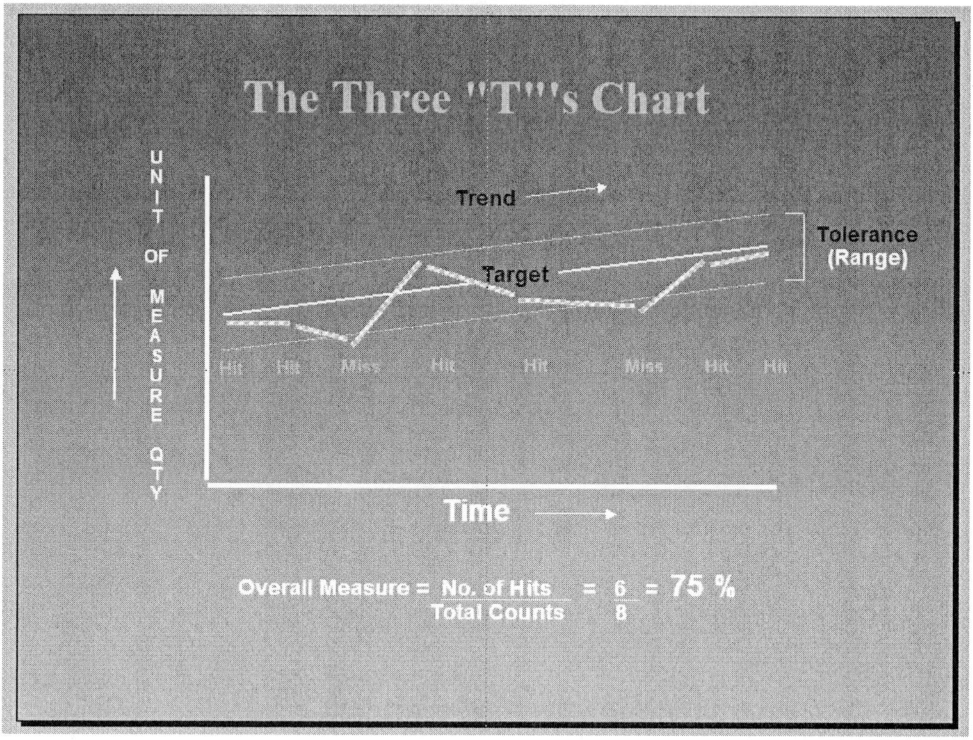

Figure 13-6 shows the charting of the "Three T's," which are Trend, Target, and Tolerance. Any measure you plot will look like this. You set the target line from wherever you are now to the end of the year.

Setting Measurement Tolerances

Figure 13-7

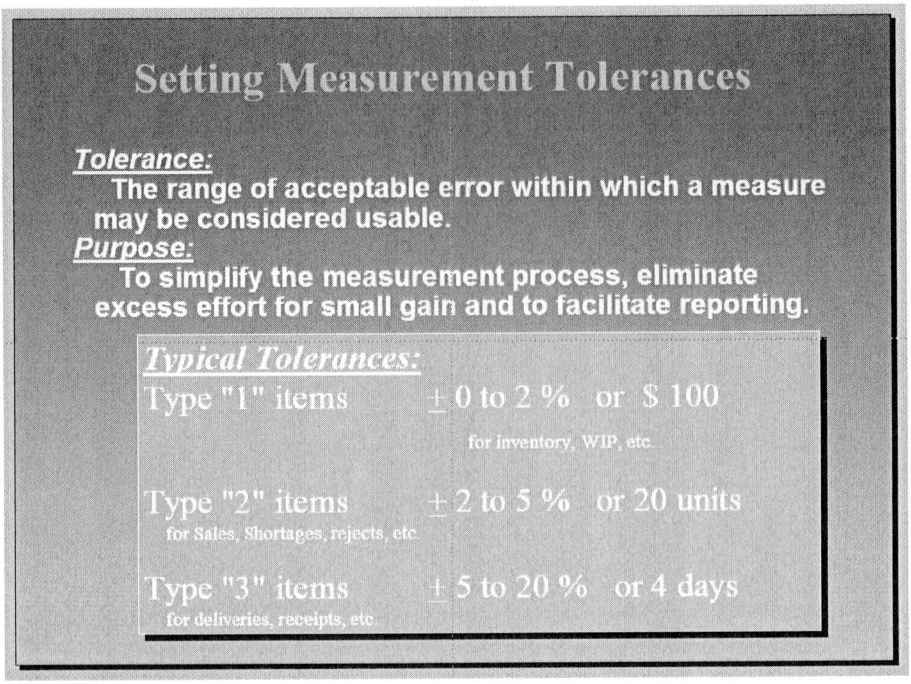

The Lean Measure Board

Figure 13-8

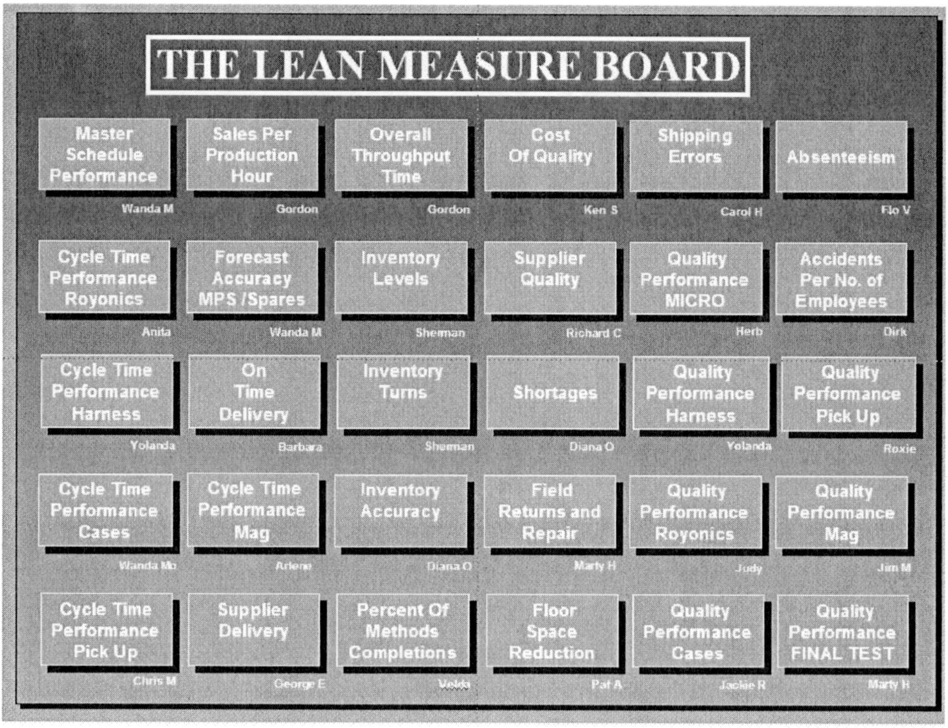

Figure 13-8 shows an example of a measure board, which publishes workers' names on a chart for everyone to see. There is a name under each one of these items. If you look at that name, then you're going to know that, say, Gordon in the second top square has our sales per production hour chart. It will tell you what your sales per an hour of production are and whether or not it improved during the year. Then, further down in another place is inventory accuracy, with Diana O. Diana O. is responsible for the inventory in the warehouse and for counting and validating the accuracies of the inventories. Her job would be to report that chart every month when it's called for on the first of the month. The entire board is mounted somewhere in an area of high traffic, such as a pathway; particularly where customers can visit it.

Inventory Turns Ratio

Figure 13-9

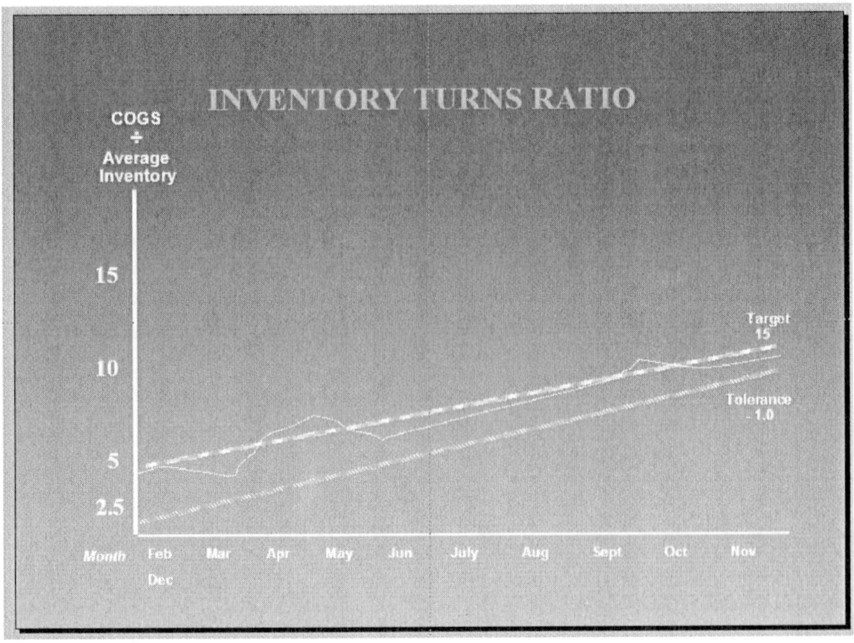

Supplier On-Time Delivery

Figure 13-10

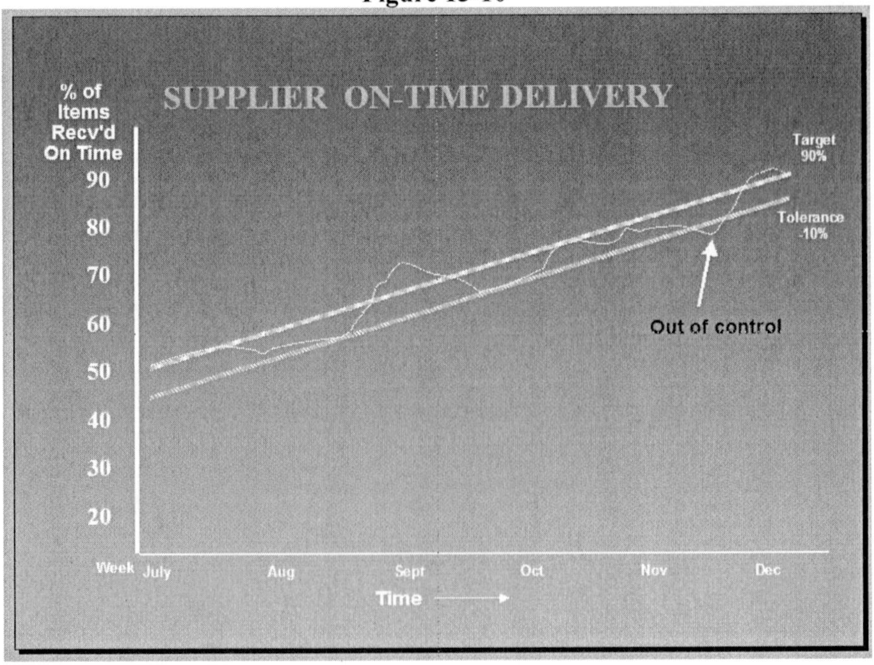

Figure 13-10 is an example of the target line, the tolerance line, and the plotted data on those two. It started off at 50 and trended up to 90. The plots varied all over the place, but, overall, only went out of control a few times. It ended up at or above the target at the end of the year. There is nothing more you need to know if you're the manager or the president of the company. If it got out of control, there was already an answer for it by the time you went into your meetings. And the names of all the people underneath this chart—like the names here—all have ownership in those measures. That's a wonderful technique because, once they have ownership, then they will tend to repeat that same positive behavior, since they have recognition for it and the achievement is noted in front of both them and others. They can see what they did, because it's right there, and they can boast of it, along with their team or the group in which they operate.

Some More Measurements

Net Profit = Profit divided by gross sales
ROI = Value of inventory vs. COGS
Cash Flow = Purchased inventory vs. shipped inventory
Customer Support = Frequency and cost of stockouts
Supplier Performance = Quality, and delivery performance
Active Inventory = Active vs. slow moving and obsolete
Space Utilization = Storage footage vs. overall square ft
Record Accuracy = Cycle count vs. book count and value
Forecast Error = Forecast vs. actual error
MPS Adherence = Quantity and dollar variance to plan
WIP Investment = WIP inventory vs. value shipped
Throughput Time= Time to pass a unit through the company

Chapter 13 Homework Assignment

1. Identify a location for a measure board within your company in a high traffic area for high visibility.
2. Using the 3T's model, generate a series of some key measures based only on this session guidelines.
3. Create at least six of the measures you would put on the Lean Measure board.

4. Try to obtain permission to mount a Lean Measure board and begin posting measures on it.
5. Identify the "owners" of each measure and post their name to the measure.
6. Do the best you can.

Chapter 13 Quiz

1. Which of the following are reasons for measurements?
A. Guard
B. Motivate
C. Pursue
D. Reply
Answer: B is correct.

2. What is the effect of seeking to meet a standard?
A. Maintenance of the status quo
B. Setting an acceptable variance
C. The tendency to motivate people
D. To calculate against
Answer: A is correct.

3. Which of the following are measures that count?
A. Efficiency, time, quality
B. Utilization, inventory and throughput
C. Time, Quality, Utilization
D. Time, Quality, Inventory
Answer: D is correct.

4. Which of the following measures are global measures for the management of the company?
A. Net Profit, ROI, On Time Billing
B. Inventory Turns, Master Schedule Improvement
C. The Cost of Quality, Inventory Levels
D. Inventory Levels, Inventory Turns, Forecast Error
Answer: C is correct.

5. What are the "Three T's"?

A. Time, Tolerance, Target
B. Target, Trend, Track
C. Tolerance, Trend, Target
D. Target, Trend, Time
Answer: C is correct.

6. The main purpose of the Lean Measure Board is to elevate ownership? True or false?
Answer: True.

Chapter 14: Kaizen and Japanese Techniques - Part A

Learning Objectives

- Define what Kaizen really does
- Discuss some Ground Rules
- Find some non-value adding events around you
- Learn the three Pillars of Kaizen
- Do an Improvement exercise

Kaizen Japanese techniques are extremely important to lean. Dr. W. Edwards Deming, a famous American quality and managerial guru, went as a young man to Japan after World War II to help develop the new country's economy. He was a statistician (mathematician). He helped to build what is now called the Japanese manufacturing systems or the Japanese operating systems, and his work formed some of the groundwork used for Kaizen. Kaizen means change, and Zen means good. So Kaizen means change for the good. There is a book called "Kaizen," by Masaaki Imai that has complete information on these Japanese techniques.

Kaizen – Change for the Good

- An incremental change system
- Defined in the gemba
- Operates within guidelines
- Autonomous within the natural work area

We're looking now at what we can do to make a change for the good in the gemba (a Japanese word for the workplace). This workplace is wherever people go to do the work they do, whether it's a general office, distribution center, sales office, or graphics department. Gemba is just where people work as groups. Just as with the theory of constraints, we're focusing on a conceptual process of continuous improvement.

Kaizen

Figure 14-1

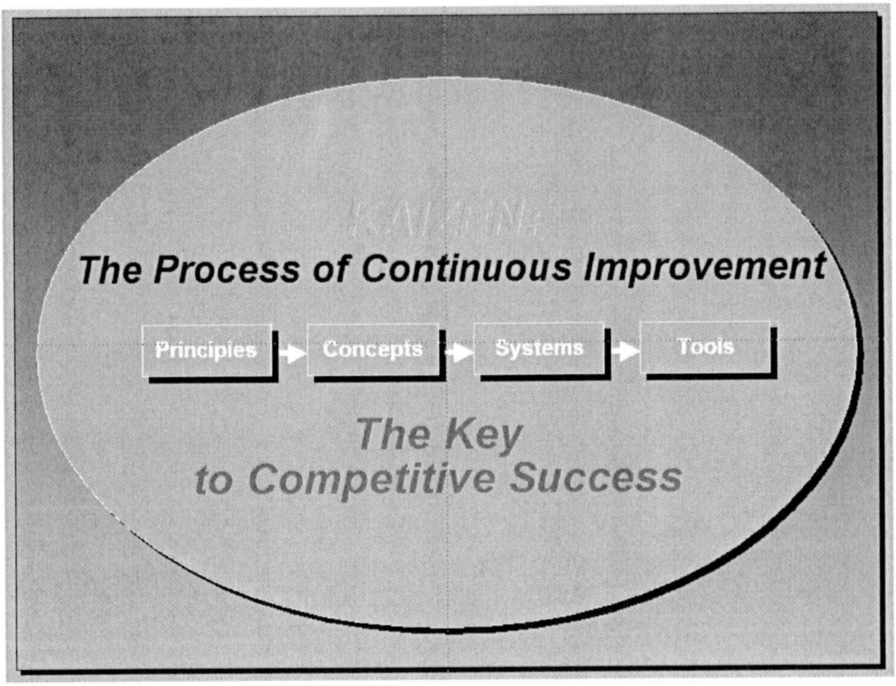

The Old and the New

Old Way to Change

- Short term results
- Task oriented
- Technique focused
- Program of the month

New Way to Change

- Long term guidance
- People oriented
- Process focus
- Consistency of purpose

The Ground Rules

- Listen and repeat
- Ask, don't tell
- Speak with data not opinions
- Focus on the topic
- No finger-pointing
- New thinking must be considered
- Do what you say you'll do
- Take risks, try a model
- Act like a pro

Continual Improvement Management

Figure 14-2

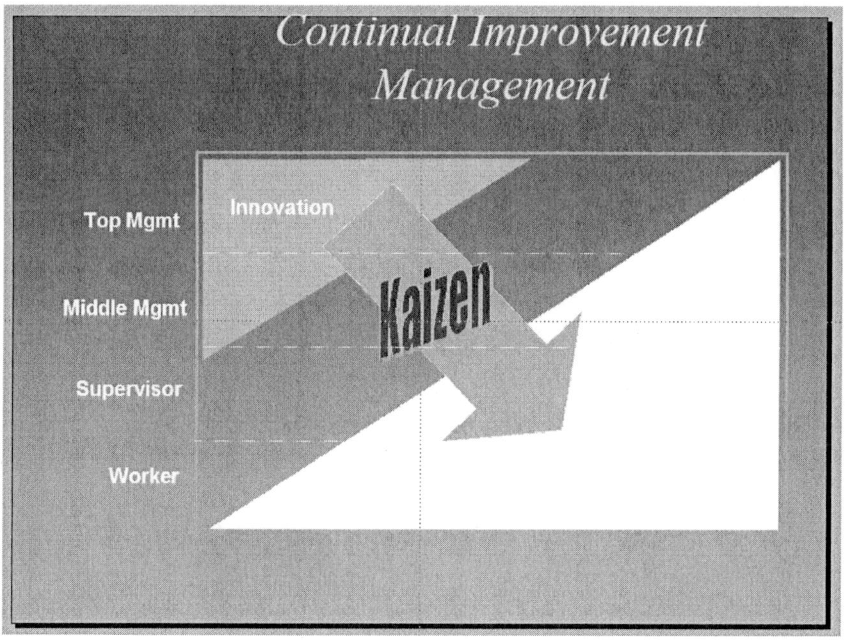

Foundation for Kaizen

Figure 14-3

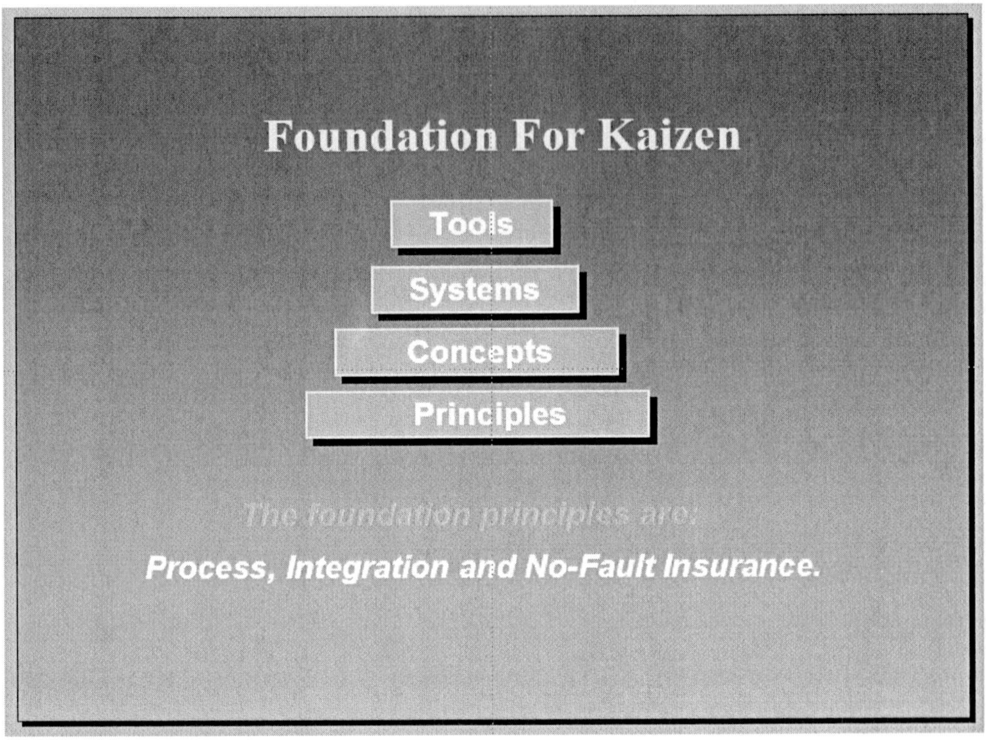

Gemba Kaizen

Figure 14-4

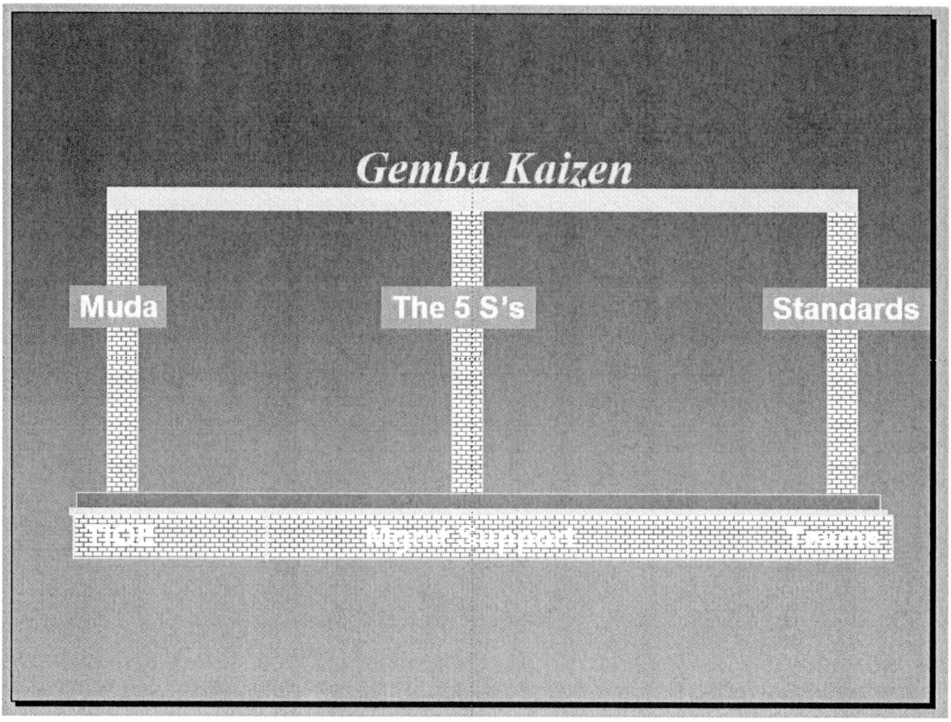

Figure 14-4 shows the three pillars of Kaizen (improvement) in the gemba (workplace). One is called Muda, which is simply a Japanese word for waste, as previously discussed.

The five S's are: sort, select, scrub, systematize, and standardize. Then you use the standards in as many places as possible. This removes a lot of waste. The whole concept is based on a foundation. On the bottom left side is TIOE, and then, on the bottom right side, is the category of teams. In the middle is management support.

The 5 Golden Rules of Gemba Kaizen

1. When a problem arises, go to gemba first
2. Check for physical evidence
3. Do temporary fixes on the spot
4. Find the root cause
5. Standardize to prevent recurrence

These are simply the rules, and they're stated very clearly: go, check, do, find, and standardize. These are action verbs. When a problem arises, go to the gemba or workplace first. Don't just hypothesize about it; go and look at the workplace and see what's going on there. It's often very easy to see it. Look for physical evidence, and make sure that there's really evidence for the things that people say. Many times people have opinions, and they somehow turn them into facts, although there's no data to support them. Do the temporary fix on the spot. Next, look for the root cause, and then standardize whatever you come up with to make sure that it continues from there after (these are standard procedures). Several books on Gemba Kaizen have been written about just these five rules.

The Sins of Muda – The 1st Pillar

1. Overproduction
2. Waiting
3. Transportation
4. Inventory
5. Waiting
6. Motion
7. Correction
8. Over-processing
9. Talents
10. Mess

Most of these have been discussed in earlier sections of this course. Talent here refers to wasted talents, i.e., people who have the ability to do something really well, but because of some glitch, the organization is not using those talents.

Example: While working at a firm, I got a master's degree. When I did, I was dying to do new things that would add value to the company, but nobody paid attention to my new talents. They paid for my education and, yet, they wouldn't let me do those new things I'd become qualified for, so I left the company. When I went somewhere else, I was promoted and got a lot more money, which means that I should have left earlier.

The last item is mess. There isn't any room in a business for mess.

Eliminating Muda from World Class Supplier Networks

• POs	• Acknowledgements
• Expediting	• Transportation Costs
• Loading/Unloading	• Counting
• Receiving Reports	• Inspection
• Sorting	• Scrap
• Supplier Returns	• Rework
• Moving	• Storage
• Repackaging	• Invoicing

The Second Pillar of Gemba Kaizen - Housekeeping

"The 5 Ss" Way of Life

1. Sort (Seiri)
   Eliminate unnecessary things
2. Straighten (Seiton)
   Everything in its place
3. Scrub (Seiso)
   Clean everything. No dirt allowed in Gemba
4. Systemize (Seiketsu)
   Routine cleaning
5. Standardize (Shitsuke)
   Habit and discipline to support the first four

The 5S principles are listed above, along with the original Japanese words from which they come. This explanation of 5S is worth a lot of money, a lot of incredible recognition, and other good things for you, if you can get people to work with you on this. It's being done as a rapidly moving program all across the U.S., Canada, and even in China. The way to implement it is as follows. Pick an area in the company that needs to have some work done. It may be some offices, shops, graphics, or crafts, etc. that need to be organized. Then you explain to everyone working there about what's going to happen. First, you're going to sort out everything that isn't necessary here, meaning that isn't going to be used for a specific period, e.g., three months. You don't need it here if it only gets used once every three months. If you have some excess area, it could be stored there, but we don't want it here in our workplace. Now, everything is out that doesn't need to be there. And then you use what's called the Red Tag technique. This is where all the group leaders and supervisors go through the area and put red stickies or tags on anything that isn't necessary. It could be that there is excess inventory, piles of pallets, an extra rack, or a truck, etc., that isn't needed there. You don't do anything about it; you just put a red tag on it. Within the next specified period, say 2 weeks, all the red tags will be removed from the workplace. This allows all work to flow through as cleanly as possible through all workplaces. You shouldn't have to go around somebody's flower pot, favorite stool and pad, or around somebody's lunch box to do the work. Those things just don't go there. It should be a clean path all the way through. People may have a problem with this. But, if we're all going to do it and management is behind it, then they will buy into that process. And if they get to tag it, they will have more ownership in changing the process. This sorting is the first step, and it is most critical.

The second step is to straighten or just basically to follow the adage that there's a place for everything. If a pencil goes in a particular place, then we put a mark for the pencil and the pencil goes there. If a trashcan goes in a specific location, then there's a circle on the floor, or a box on the wall, that says trash or basura (in Spanish) and that's where the trashcan goes. So, anytime anybody's walking through the area, including the boss and the workers, they all know that the item goes in its specific place, not anywhere else.

The next step, of course, is to scrub, and that means everybody—the bosses, supervisors, "kings" and "queens," no matter who they are. They all need to be cleaning, scrubbing, painting, labeling, marking, and otherwise making the workplace so that it's a really lovely place to see.

Example from Dennis Fisher: I was working with a worldwide gear manufacturing company. When I walked through the factory to see the way they made the gears, bearings, and related products, I had to step very carefully. There was a lot of slippery oil on the floor, so I couldn't put my heel down first; I had to walk flat like a penguin or something. Most of the plant was like that. Also, wherever I walked, there was oil floating in the air. It was a mess. At the other end of that plant was another one of their groups, and they made bearings for nuclear reactors and motors. When I went down to that end and got to their door, it had an air vacuum door and filters. The floors were white. It was exciting! Everybody in there had on a nice clean smock. They were making the same bearings that they were making down on the other end, except that it was in a clean environment.

The next step is to systematize. All of the cleaning, organizing, and structuring should be set in stone. The first shift does this cleaning, second shift does that one, third shift does another, etc. We rotate these people to make sure that everybody has their fair share and that it doesn't overburden to anybody. Systematizing is a routine that keeps going.

The final step is to standardize. This is where all of the changes just become a way of life. It becomes just what you do. You don't throw stuff on the floor anywhere. Every worker knows, "We have a dispenser for that." And everybody in the company knows you don't go into that clean end and make a mess. You don't drop anything, and you wipe your feet off before you go in. That's just the way it is, and nobody even questions it. This makes a great work environment.

Example: In one of the companies previously mentioned, the simple application of 5S moved 75% of the inventory out of the system and out of the warehouse. It was a marvelous addition to space. They took out a complete set of racks that was high, long, wide, and filled with junk—and just got rid of it all. It was stuff that people had collected over decades. When it was done, there was faster throughput, higher productivity, and a smaller amount of floor space. This let them use more floor space for other productive work, and they needed one person less out of seven people. So the displaced worker went to another department that needed somebody. Yet there was more productivity. All of that came from implementing 5S only.

Five Simple Kaizen Tools

1. Poka-Yoke
Fail-Safe mechanisms.
2. The 5 "S's
Clean and organize the workplace
3. Low-Cost Automation - Jidoka

Cheap, movable machines with automatic moves.
4. Muda Reduction
Eliminate all muda
5. Set-up Reduction
Convert internals to externals.

Improvement Exercise

1. Form two large groups.
2. Select an item for improvement to pass through your group.
3. Check time and distance to travel around the group.
4. Look at the process flow.
5. Determine a faster, shorter process.
6. Do it again, and again until its distance and process time has decreased by at least 75%.
7. Compare the performance of the two groups.

Chapter 14 Homework Assignment 1

List at least two actions they you will take to apply one or more Kaizen elements in the gemba:
1.
2.

Chapter 14 Homework Assignment 2

1. Identify a location for a measure board within your company in a high traffic area for high visibility.
2. Using the 3T's model, generate a series of some key measures based only on this section's guidelines.
3. Create at least six of the measures you would put on the lean measure board.
4. Try to obtain permission to mount a lean measure board and begin posting measures on it.
5. Identify the "owners" of each measure and post their name to the measure.
6. Do the best you can.

Chapter 14 Quiz

1. What is the meaning and purpose of Kaizen?
A. Changing the good
B. It's good to change
C. Change for the good
D. Good can change
Answer: C is correct.

2. Which of the following are the three pillars of Kaizen?
A. Standards, Change, 5S
B. Change, 5S, Muda
C. Waste, 5S, Standards
D. Standards, Muda, Waste
Answer: C is correct.

3. Lot size reduction is NOT one of the Kaizen techniques. True or false?
Answer: False.

4. One of the 5 golden rules of Gemba Kaizen is that when a problem arises, you should go to Gemba first. True or false?
Answer: True.

5. Eliminating moving is the most effective Sin of Muda to eliminate. True or false?
Answer: True.

6. Which of the following are the 3 main foundations Kaizen? (Choose all that apply.)
A. Process, Integration, and No-Fault Insurance
B. Input, Process, and Output
C. Blame, Accountability, and Pay
D. None of the above
Answer: A is correct.

Chapter 15: Kaizen and Japanese Techniques Part B

Learning Objectives

- Define the 3rd Pillar of Gemba Kaizen.
- List and select your favorite Kaizen rules.
- Review what Lean systems have actually done for the world.

Standardization - The 3rd Pillar of Gemba Kaizen

1. The best, safest, easiest way
2. That preserves the knowledge learned
3. That can be measured
4. That shows cause and effect
5. That is the baseline for future improvements
6. That provides objectives
7. That can be audited

Standardizing is really quite simple, but somebody has to do the work.

Example: I worked with a well-known company that made large data storage devices (terabytes in volume). We set up a manufacturing operation to make standardized turnaround containers. We started with a big plywood box, about 8 feet long and about 2 feet wide. It had a front door flap that would drop down and some shelves. It also had little pukas (segments) in each part that would hold 10 parts of each of the assembly that would be on this product line. We had four of these boxes made. For each assembly of each product made, they would take one of a particular part, and then one of another, and another of those from the top and around the side, etc. When they had used all of those up completely, making 10 units for 10 sets of each, then that would roll out to the back door, which was maybe 60 feet away, and they'd pick up a new one there. It was a Kanban (signaled) location. So, there was a full one sitting there and an empty one. Then they would bring in that box, move it up here, place it down, and 10 new, exactly matching parts were available. Then they would make another 10 units. And when that unit of 10 was finished, this box would roll out. The supplier would come, drop off another box, and pick up the old box, so that there was a new one there. And they would make another one at their factory. So there were four boxes needed. That kept us going for a couple of days at a time for each box. That's standardizing. It required no brains, no thinking, no analyzing, no calculating and, when you opened it up, they were either there or they were not. If you damaged one you would be in trouble, because we couldn't just get one. Actually, you could, but you don't want to go through all the effort.

Standardization (Plan)

Figure 15-1

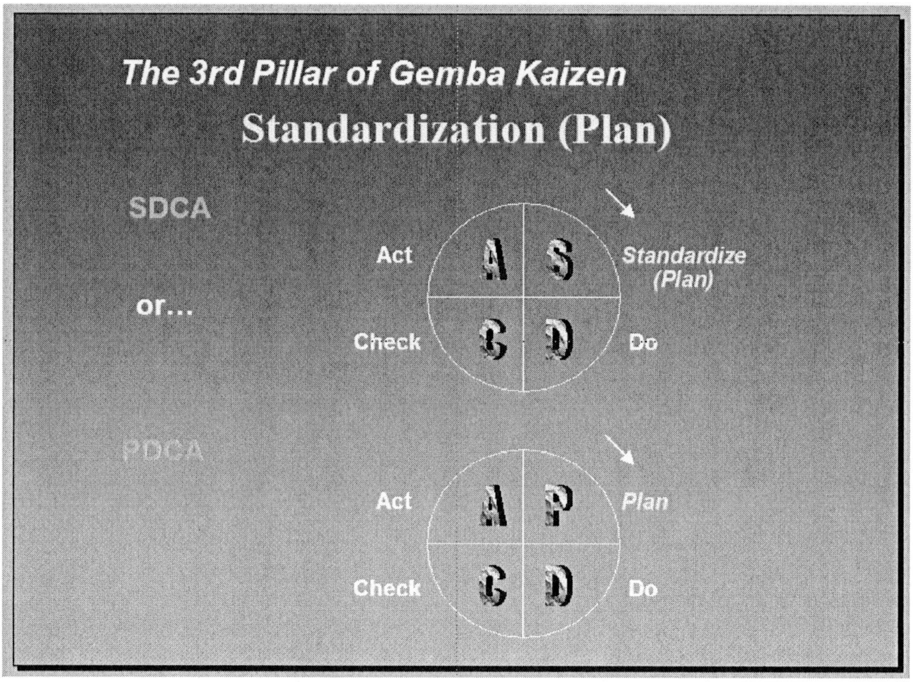

Dr. Deming was instrumental in developing a technique called the PDCA or PDSA, which stands for plan, do, check, act; or plan, do, study, act. It's basically about having a consistently repetitive way of presenting an improvement project. In Kaizen, the method is called storyboarding. Figure 15-1 shows a Kaizen storyboard. For example, somebody comes in saying, "Hey, look, this thing is broken—we've got to fix it or replace it." So you ask the three questions of TIOE. Then they all say, "Yeah, that works so that's what we're going to do." Now, we're going to set up a plan to go about changing it. Here is the layout of that plan. First we're going to decide what the theme is. We ask ourselves, "What are we going to do here?" The answer must be that we're going to improve throughput through the specific target department. Then, we're going to look at the checkpoints, the working plan measures, the goals and problems and define it at the front end. But these are the only questions that need to be answered. This makes you think out the whole process.

Then, when that's done, the next thing you will show in your PDCA or plan, do, check, act, is going to be the part about doing the work or changes. So, you start doing whatever that thing is: move something, put a desk over here, put a window over there, etc. Next, you go to check or study—plan, do, study, act or plan, do, check, act. Analyze the data and search for root causes of processes that are wandering off target or that aren't working. You have some statistical process control (SPC) here, or you have some tools that are coming out of sigma. Basically, the standard statistical tools could be used for doing research here on the work you just did. Plan, do, check. Then, the last part, which is, of course, the one you'd like to get to—is act. This is where we turn whatever we did into a permanent policy. We have retrained and implemented the new procedures. And then, in order to prevent any failure, we're going to go back and do another one. We'll just keep on rolling from plan, do, check, act to plan, do, check act.

So we first saw the bottleneck. Then we did the TIOE. Next, we did the PDCA. Following that, we went back and started all over again--a continuous improvement forever and ever. Everyday you come to work it's different, exciting, and a new way to work, as opposed to the way it used to be, where it was dull, boring, and repetitive.

SDCA - "The Kaizen Storyboard"
Standardize

Figure 15-2

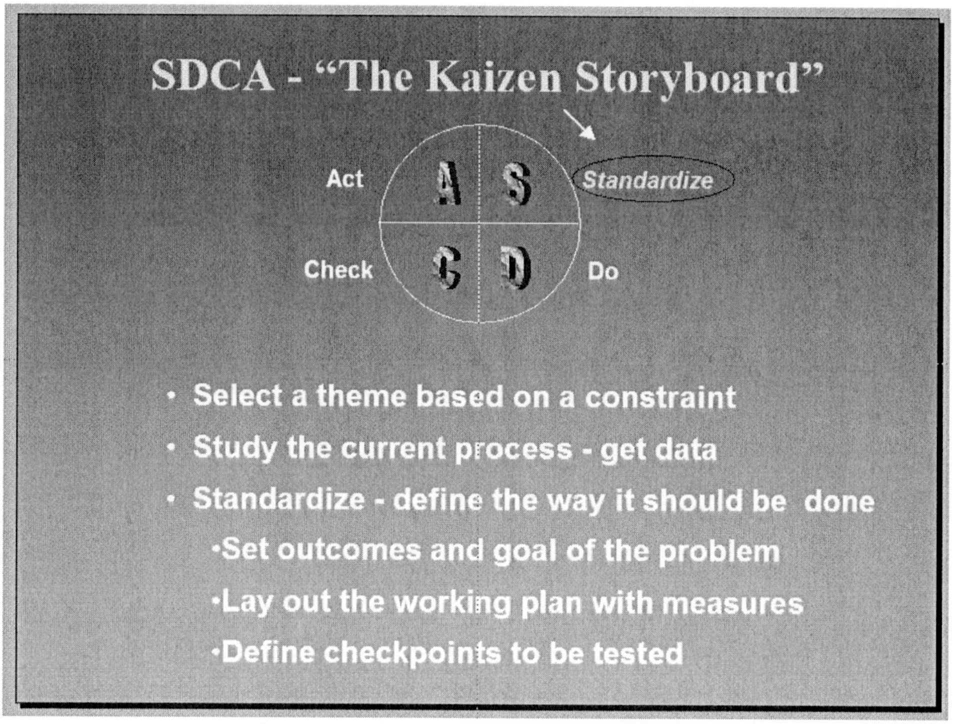

SDCA - "The Kaizen Storyboard" - Do
Figure 15-3

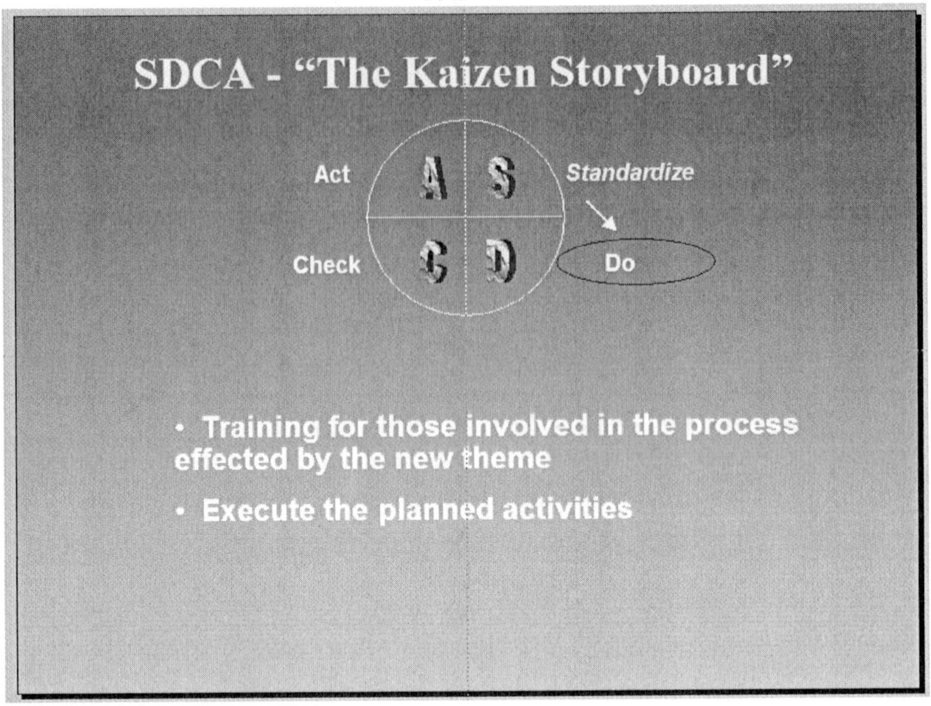

SDCA - "The Kaizen Storyboard" - Check

Figure 15-4

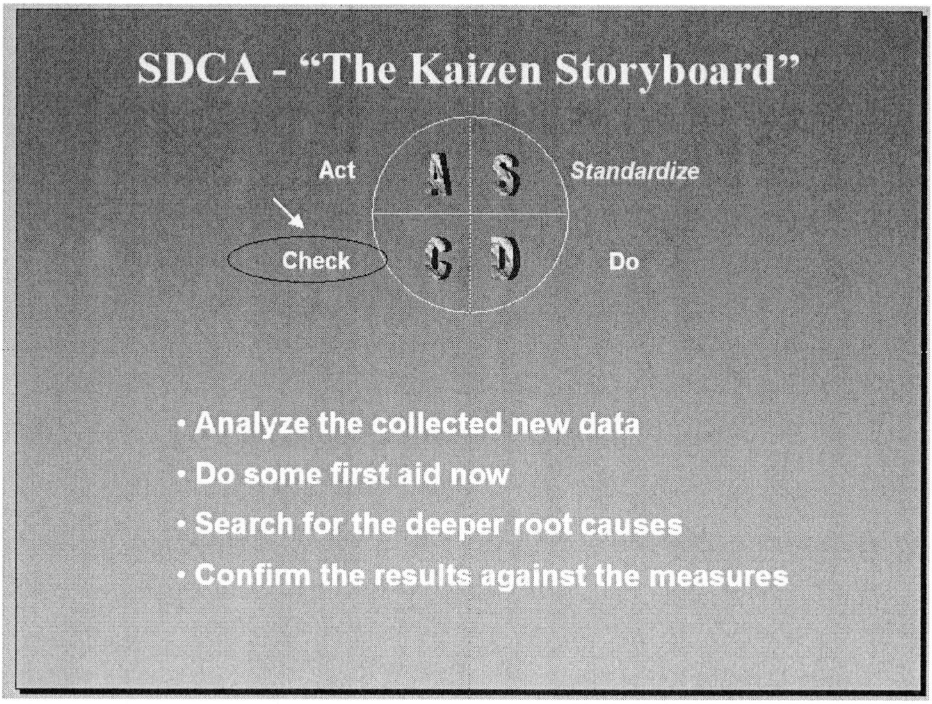

SDCA - "The Kaizen Storyboard" - Act

Figure 15-5

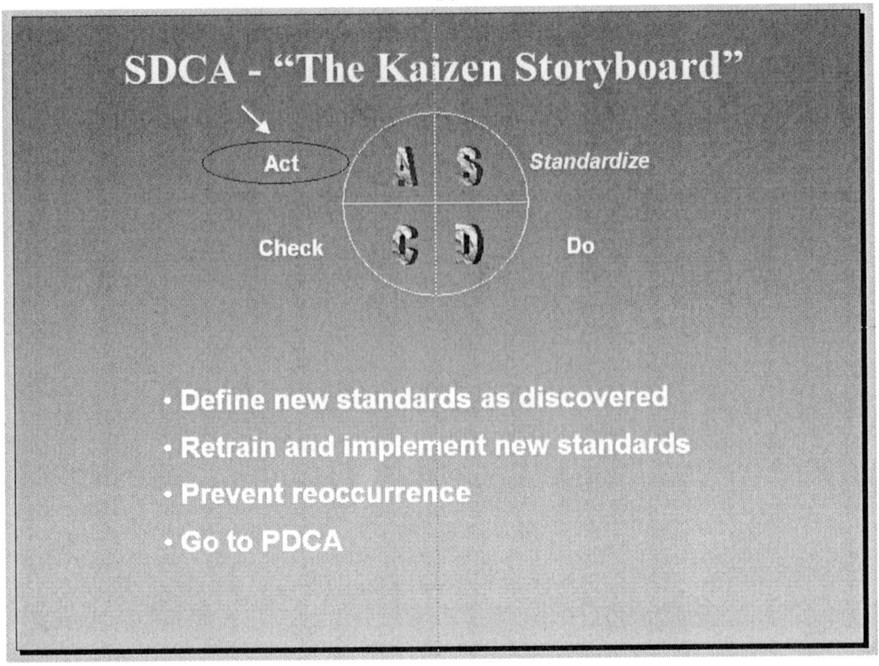

PDCA - "The Kaizen Storyboard" – Plan

Figure 15-6

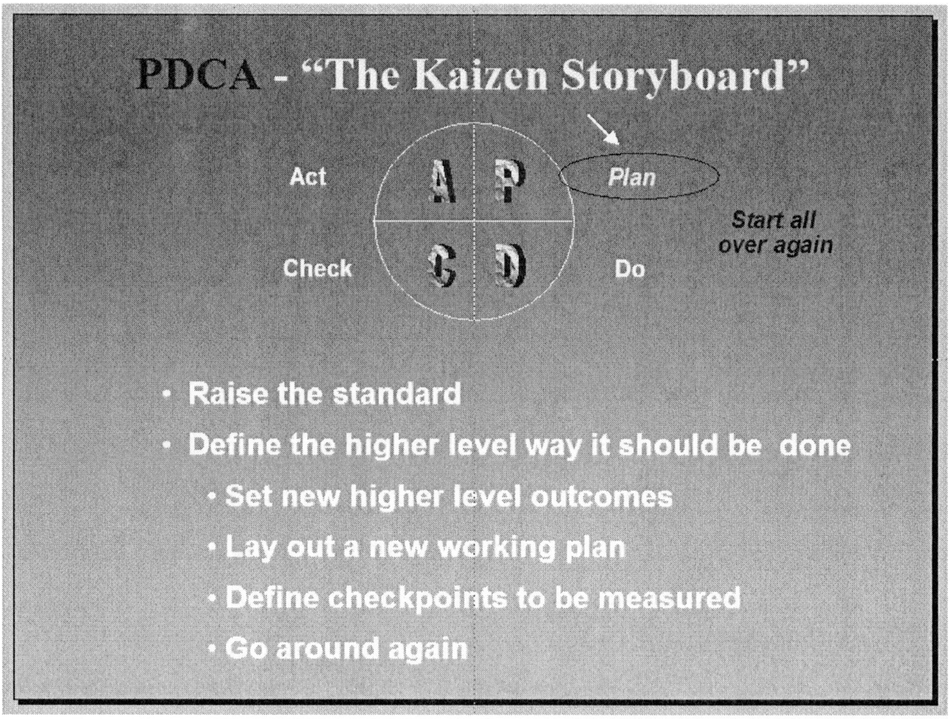

From SDCA to PDCA

Figure 15-7

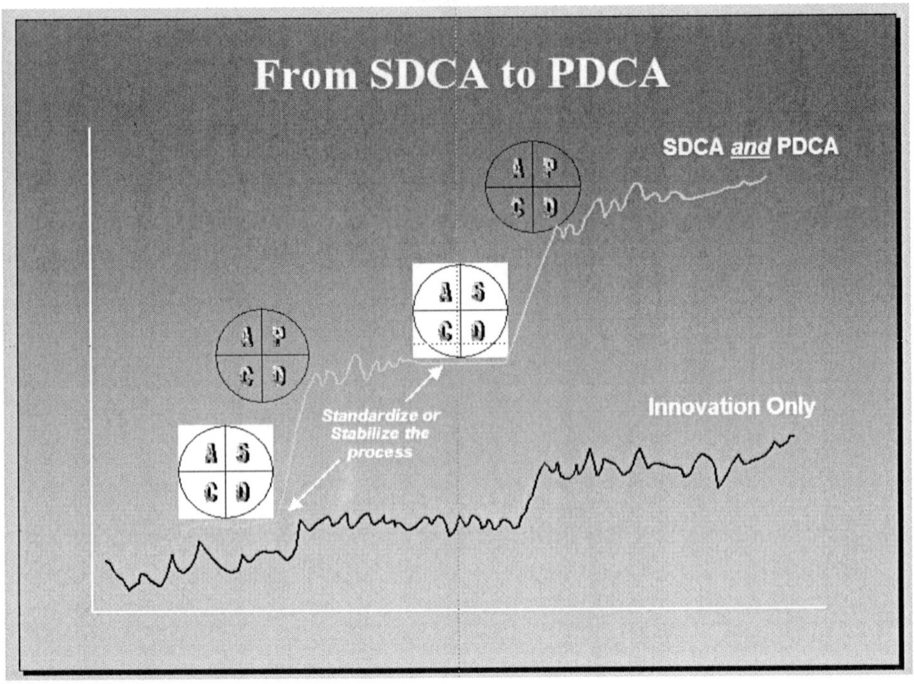

The Ten Basic Rules for Kaizen

1. Stop rigid thinking about production.
2. Think of how to do it; not why it can't be done.
3. Don't make excuses about why you can't do it.
4. Don't seek perfection, just do it now for less than the maximum benefit.
5. Don't spend any money for Kaizen.
6. Ask why 5 times and search for the root cause.
7. Seek the wisdom of ten, not the knowledge of one.
8. Remember the opportunities for Kaizen are endless.
9. Wisdom is revealed when facing hardship
10. Correct mistakes at once.

Comparable Lean Performances

Figure 15-8

Comparable Lean Performances*

Issue	*Toyota*	*Japan*	*USA*	*Europe*
Productivity	100	83	65	54
Quality Defects Per Car	30	55	61	61
Delivery on Time Suppliers	99.6%	98%	94%	81%
Inventory Turns	248	81	69	45

•Lean Thinking, Womack and Jones; Auto Assembly Manufacturing, 1996

Chapter 15 Homework Assignment

1. Identify a problem or project for improvement (based on TIOE).
2. Write a clear definition and purpose (results) for the problem.
3. Lay out a Kaizen Storyboard or SDCA using the content of this lesson to define each step in the cycle.

Chapter 15 Quiz

1. What is the 3rd Pillar of Kaizen?
A. Waste
B. Standardization
C. Throughput
D. Cost
Answer: B is correct.

2. What does "standardize" mean in the building of a Storyboard?
A. Maintenance of the status quo

B. Setting an acceptable variance
C. To motivate people to repeat the same behavior
D. To lay out a defined approach to a specific Improvement
Answer: A is correct.

3. Which of the four steps 1n the PDCA/SDCA Storyboard have measures?
A. P
B. D
C. C
D. A
Answer: D is correct.

4. Which of the 10 Basic Rules for Kaizen would be done several times?
A. Don't make excuses about why you can't do it
B. Seek the wisdom of ten, not the knowledge of one
C. Ask why 5 times and search for the root cause
D. Don't seek perfection, just do it now for less than the maximum benefit.
Answer: C is correct.

5. What lesson is seen in comparable data between Europe, USA, and Japan?
A. That USA's performance is somewhere between EU and Japan.
B. That Toyota is better than everyone
C. That Japan is better than USA and EU
D. All the above
Answer: C is correct.

6. A Kaizen Storyboard's purpose is to accommodate employee problems. True or false?
Answer: False. Its purpose is to elevate ownership.

Appendix A: Lean Glossary

Aggregate inventory - The inventory for any groupings of items or products involving multiple stock-keeping units.
Algorithm - A prescribed set of well-defined rules or processes for the solution of a problem in a finite number.
Allocation - In an MRP system, an allocated item is one for which a picking order has been released to the stockroom but not yet sent out of the stockroom. It is an uncached stockroom requisition. It can also be a process used to distribute material in short supply.
Alpha factor - The smoothing constant applied to the most recent forecast error in exponential smoothing forecasting.
Anticipation inventories - Additional inventory above basic stocking levels to cover projected increasing trends of sales, planned sales promotion programs, seasonal fluctuations, plant shutdowns, price changes, shortages and vacations.
Assemble-to-order product - A make-to-order product where all components (bulk semi-finished, intermediate, subassembly, fabricated, purchased, packaging, etc.) used in the assembly, packaging, or finishing process are planned and stocked in anticipation of a customer order. See make-to-order product.
Assembly - A group of subassemblies and/or parts that are put together and constitute a major subdivision for the final product. An assembly may be an end item or a component of a higher-level assembly. See component; subassembly.
Automated storage/retrieval system - A high-density rack storage system with vehicles automatically loading and unloading the racks.
Available inventory - The on-hand balance minus allocations, reservations, backorders, and (usually) quantities held for quality problems. Often called "beginning available balance."
Available to promise - The uncommitted portion of a company's inventory or planned production. This figure is normally calculated from the master production schedule plus the beginning balance in the first planning period less all customer orders before the next master schedule receipt. It is used as a tool for customer order promising in assemble-to-. order and make-to-order operations.
Average forecast error - The arithmetic mean of the forecast errors, or the exponentially smoothed forecast error. See forecast error; mean absolute deviation.

Backflush - The deduction from inventory of the component parts used in an assembly or subassembly by exploding the bill of materials by the production count of products or assemblies produced. Synonym: post-deduct inventory transaction processing or theoretical consumption. See single-level backflush; superflush.

Backlog - All of the customer orders received but not yet shipped. Sometimes referred to as "open orders" or the "order board."

Backorder - An unfilled customer order or commitment. It is an immediate (or past due) demand against an item whose inventory is insufficient to satisfy the demand. See stockout.

Back scheduling - A technique for calculating operation start and due dates. The schedule is computed starting with the due date for the order and working backward to determine the required start date and/or due dates for each operation.

Balancing operations - In repetitive Just-In-Time production, trying to match actual output cycle times of all operations to the demand of use for parts as required by final assembly and eventually as required by the market.

Bar coding - A method of encoding data for fast and accurate readability. Bar codes are a series of wide or narrow, light or dark, vertically printed lines where the width of lines and spaces between lines is arranged to represent letters and numbers.

Beginning inventory - A statement of the inventory count at the end of last period, usually from a perpetual inventory record.

Bill of labor - See product load profile.

Bill of material (BOM) - A listing of all the subassemblies, intermediates, parts, and raw materials that go into a parent assembly showing the quantity of each required to make an assembly. There are a variety of display formats of bill of material, including single level bill of material, indented bill of material, modular (planning) bill of material, transient bill of material, matrix bill of material, costed bill of material, etc. May also be called "formula," "recipe," "ingredients list" in certain industries.

Bill of material structuring - The process of organizing bills of material to perform specific functions. See bill of material, planning bill.

Bill of resources - See product load profile.

Blanket order - A long-term commitment to a vendor for material against which short-term releases will be generated to satisfy requirements. Often blanket orders cover only one item, with predetermined delivery dates.

Blow-through - See phantom bill of material.

Bottleneck - A facility, function, department, and so on that impedes production—for example, a machine or work center where jobs arrive at a faster rate than they can be completed.

bucketless system - An MRP, DRP, or other time-phased system in which all time-changed dates are processed, stored, and usually displayed using dated records rather than defined time periods or "buckets." See bucketed system, time bucket.

Burden - Costs incurred in the operation of a business that can be directly related to the individual work centers for products or services produced. These costs, such as power consumption, indirect labor, engineering support, and set-up people, are charged or allocated directly to the work center that employs them. These costs are then distributed to units of product, or service, by allocating the proportion of costs that were used by any product or service flowing through that work center. This is the basis of activity based costing.

Capacity - (1) In a general sense, refers to an aggregated volume of workload. It is a separate concept from priority. See priority. (2) The highest reasonable output rate that can be achieved with the current product specifications, product mix, work force, plant, and equipment.

Capacity requirement planning (CRP) - The function of establishing, measuring, and adjusting limits or levels of capacity. The term capacity requirements planning in this context is the process of determining how much labor and machine resources are required to accomplish the tasks of production. Open shop orders, and planned orders in the MRP system, are input to CRP, which "translates" these orders into hours of work by work center by time period. See infinite loading, closed-loop MRP; rough cut capacity planning.

Carrying cost - Cost of carrying inventory, usually defined as a percent of the dollar value of inventory per unit of time (generally one year). Depends mainly on cost of capital invested as well as the costs of maintaining the inventory, such as taxes and insurance, obsolescence, spoilage, and space occupied. Such costs vary from 10-35 percent annually, depending on type of industry. Ultimately, carrying cost is a policy variable reflecting the opportunity cost alternative uses for funds tied up in inventory. See economic order quantity; cost of capital.

Cause and Effect Diagram - A precise statement of a problem or phenomenon with a branching diagram leading from the statement to the known potential causes. Synonym: fishbone chart, Ishikawa diagram.

Cellular Manufacturing - A manufacturing process that produces fami-

lies of parts within a single line or cell of machines operated by machinists who work only within the line or cell.
Centralized dispatching - Organization of the dispatching function into one central location. This often involves the use of data collection devices for communication between the centralized dispatching function, which usually reports to the production control department, and the shop manufacturing departments. See decentralized dispatching.
Changeover - The refitting of equipment to either neutralize the effects of the just completed production, to prepare the equipment for production of the next scheduled item, or both. See setup.
Changeover cost - The sum of the teardown costs and the setup costs for a manufacturing operation. See idle time. Synonym: turnaround costs; shutdown/startup costs.
Closed-loop MRP - A system built around material requirement planning and also including the additional planning functions of sales and operations (production planning, master production scheduling, and capacity requirements planning). Further, once this planning phase is complete and the plans have been accepted as realistic and attainable, the execution functions come into play. These include the manufacturing control functions of input-output measurement, detailed scheduling and dispatching, as well as anticipated delay reports from both the plant and vendors, vendor scheduling, etc. The term closed-loop implies that not only is each of these elements included in the overall system but also that there is feedback from the execution functions so the planning can be kept valid at all times. See: manufacturing resource planning.
Commodity buying - Grouping like parts or materials under one buyer's control for the procurement of all requirements to support production.
Component - A term used to identify a raw material, ingredient, part, or subassembly that goes into a high-level assembly, compound, or other item. May also include packaging materials for finished items. See assembly.
Composite part - A part that represents operations common to a family or group of parts controlled by group technology. Tools, jigs, and dies are used for the composite part and, therefore, any parts of that family cart be processed with the same operations and tooling. The goal here is to reduce setup costs. See group technology.
Computer aided design (CAD) - The use of computers in interactive engineering drawing and storage of designs. Programs complete that layout, geometric transformations, projections, rotations, magnifications,

and interval (cross-section) views of a part and its relationship with other parts.

Computer aided manufacturing (CAM) - Use of computers to program, direct, and control production equipment in the fabrication of manufactured items.

Computer numerical control (CNC) - A technique in which a machine tool control uses a minicomputer to store numerical instructions.

Consigned stocks - Inventories, generally of finished products, that are in the possession of customers, dealers, agents, etc., but remain the property of the manufacturer by agreement with those in possession.

Constraint - A limitation placed on the maximization or minimization of a objective function. These usually result from scarcity of the resources necessary for attaining some objective. See objective function. Synonym: structural constraint; restriction.

Continuous production - A production system in which the productive equipment is organized and sequenced according to the steps involved to produce the product. Denotes that material flow is continuous during the production process. The routing of the jobs is fixed-and setups are seldom changed. See intermittent production.

Control chart - A statistical device usually used for the study and control of repetitive processes. It is designed to reveal the randomness or non-randomness of deviations from a mean or control value, usually by plotting these.

Cost center - The smallest segment of an organization for which costs are collected, typically a department. The criteria in defining cost centers are that the cost be significant and the area of responsibility be clearly defined. A cost center may not be identical to a work center. Normally, it would encompass more than one work center. See work center.

Cost of capital - The cost of maintaining a dollar of capital invested for a certain period, normally one year. This cost is normally expressed as a percentage and may be based on such factors as the average expected return on alternative investments and current bank interest rate for borrowing. See economic order quantity.

Critical path method (CPM) - A network planning technique used for planning and controlling the activities in a project. By showing each of these activities and their associated times, the "critical path" can be determined. The critical path identifies elements that actually constrain the total time for the project. See PERT.

Cumulative lead-time - The longest planned length of time involved to accomplish the activity in question. For any item planned through MRP, it is found by reviewing the lead-time for each bill of material path below the item. Whichever path adds up to the greatest number defines cumulative lead-time. Synonym: aggregate lead-time; stacked lead-time; composite lead time; critical path lead time; and combined lead time.

Cycle - (1) The interval of time during which a system or process, such as seasonal demand or a manufacturing operation, periodically returns to similar initial conditions. In inventory control, a cycle is often taken to be the length of time between two replenishment shipments. (2) The interval of time during which an event or set of events is completed. In production control, a cycle is often taken to be the length of time between the release of a manufacturing order and shipment to the customer or inventory. Synonym: manufacturing cycle; manufacturing lead time.

Cycle counting - An inventory accuracy audit technique where inventory is counted on a cyclic schedule, rather than once a year. For example, a cycle inventory count is usually taken on a regular, defined basis (often more frequently for high-value fast-moving items and less frequently for low-value or slow-moving items). Most effective cycle counting systems require the counting of a certain number of items every workday with each item counted at a prescribed frequency. The key purpose of cycle counting is to identify items in error, thus triggering research, identification, and elimination of the cause of the errors. See ABC classification.

Cycle stock - One of the four main components of any item inventory, the cycle stock is the most active part; (i.e., that which depletes gradually and is replenished cyclically when orders are received). See lot size.

Cycle time - (1) In industrial engineering, the time between completion of two discrete units of production. For example, the cycle time of motors assembled at a rate of 120 per hour would be 30 seconds, or one every half minute. (2) In materials management, it refers to the length of time from when material enters a production facility until it exists. Synonym: throughput time.

Data - Any representations, such as alphabetic or numeric characters, to which meaning can be assigned. See information.

Data base - A data processing file-management approach designed to establish the independence of computer programs from data files. Redundancy is minimized and data elements can be added to or deleted from the file designs without necessitating changes to existing computer programs.

Dedicated line - A production line "permanently" configured to run well-

defined parts, one piece at a time from station to station.
Delivery lead-time - The time from the receipt of the customer order to the delivery of the product. Synonym: delivery cycle. See lead-time.
Delivery schedule - The required and/or agreed time or rate of delivery of goods or services purchased for a future period.
Demand - A need for a particular product or component. The demand could come from any number of sources, (i.e., customer order, forecast, interplant, branch warehouse, service part, or for manufacturing another product). At the finished goods level, "demand data" are usually different from "sales data" because demand does not necessarily result in sales, (i.e., if there is no stock there will be no sale). See: dependent demand; independent demand.
Demand filter - A standard set to monitor individual sales data in forecasting models. Usually set to be tripped when the demand for a period differs from the forecast by more than some number of mean absolute deviations.
Demand management - The function of recognizing and managing all of the demands for products to ensure that the master scheduler is aware of them. It encompasses the activities of forecasting, order entry, order promising, branch warehouse requirements, interplant orders, and service parts requirements. See master production schedule.
Demand pull - The triggering of material movement to a work center only when that work center is out of work and/or ready to begin the next job. It in effect eliminates queues from a front of a work center, but it can cause queues at the end of a previous work center. See pull.
Demonstrated capacity - Proven capacity calculated from actual output performance data, usually number of items produced times standard hours per item. Synonym: actual capacity. See rated capacity.
Dependent demand - Demand is considered dependent when it is directly related to or derived from the schedule for other items or end products. Such demands, therefore, are calculated and need not and should not be forecast. A given inventory item may have both dependent and independent demand at any given time. See independent demand.
Deterioration - Product spoilage, damage to the package, and the like. One of the considerations is inventory carrying cost. See obsolescence.
Deviation - The difference, usually the absolute difference, between a number and the mean of a set of numbers, or between a forecast value and the actual datum.
Direct cost - A variable cost that can be directly attributed to a particular

job or operation. See: variable cost.

Direct labor - Labor specifically applied to the product being manufactured or utilized in the performance of the service.

Direct material - Materials which become a part of the final product in measurable quantities. See indirect materials.

Discrete manufacturing - Production of distinct items: automobiles, appliances, computers. See process manufacturing.

Distribution requirements planning - The function of determining the needs to replenish inventory at branch warehouses. A time-phased order point approach is used, where the planned orders at the branch warehouse level are "exploded" via MRP logic to become gross requirements on the supplying source. In the case of multilevel distribution networks, this explosion process can continue down through the various levels of master warehouse, factory warehouse, and so on, and become input to the master production schedule. Demand on the supplying source(s) is recognized as dependent, and standard MRP logic applies. See time-phased order point; physical distribution; push (distribution system).

Downstream operation - Subsequent tasks to the task currently being planned or executed.

Downtime - Time when a machine is scheduled for operation but is not producing for such reasons as maintenance, repair, or setup.

Due date - The date when purchased material or production material is due to be available for use. See need date; scheduled receipt.

Dynamic lot sizing - A lot-sizing technique that creates an order quantity subject to continuous recomputation. See least total cost; least unit cost; part period balancing; period order quantity.

Economic Order Quantity (EOQ) - A type of fixed order quantity, which determines the amount of an item to be purchased or manufactured at one time. The intent is to minimize the combined costs of acquiring and carrying inventory.

Efficiency - Standard hours earned divided by actual hours worked. Efficiency is a measure of how closely predetermined standards are achieved. Efficiency for a given time can be calculated for a machine, an employee, a group of machines, a department, and so on.

Electronic data interchange (EDI) - The paperless (electronic) exchange of trading documents such as purchase orders, shipment authorizations, advance shipment notices, invoices, or sales orders using standardization document formats. EDI is used mostly between businesses and institutions with different computer systems.

Ending inventory - A statement of on-hand quantities at the end of a period, often determined by a physical inventory. See beginning inventory.
Engineering change - A revision to a parts list, bill of material, or drawings authorized by the engineering department. Changes are usually identified by a control number and are made for safety, cost reduction, functionality, or process improvement reasons. To effectively implement engineering changes, all affected functions, such as materials, purchasing, quality assurance, and assembly engineering, should review and agree to the changes.
Engineer-to-order - Products whose customer specifications require unique engineering design or significant customization. Each customer order then results in a unique set of part numbers, bills of material, and routings.
Exception report - A report that lists or flags only those items deviating from plan.
Expediting - The "rushing" or "chasing" of production or purchase orders that are needed in less than the normal lead time. In program review and evaluation technique (PERT), expediting is to track and report performance of each step in the process to determine if the project is on track, compared to a "critical path" of the longest lead time item sequence. See dispatching.
Exponential smoothing - A type of weighted moving average forecasting technique in which past observations are geometrically discounted according to their age. The heaviest weight is assigned to the most recent data. The smoothing is termed exponential because data points are weighted in accordance with an exponential function of their age. The technique makes use of a smoothing constant to apply to the difference between the most recent forecast and the critical sales data, that avoids the necessity of carrying historical sales data. The approach can be used for data that exhibit no trend or seasonal patterns or for data with either (or both) trend and seasonality.
Exposures - The number of times per year that the system risks a stock out. This number of exposures is derived by dividing the lot size into the annual usage. Theoretically, the smaller the lot size the larger the number of exposures to a stock out.
External setup time - Elements of a setup procedure performed while the process is in production; the machine is running. See internal setup time.
Extrinsic forecast - A forecast based on a correlated leading indicator or indices such as estimating furniture sales based on housing starts.

Extrinsic forecasts tend to be more useful for large aggregations, such as total company sales or product groups, than for individual product sales. Ant: intrinsic forecasts.

Fabrication - A term used to distinguish manufacturing operations for components, as opposed to assembly operations.

Failsafe work methods - Methods of performing operations so incorrect actions cannot be completed. Examples: part without holes in the proper place cannot be removed from a jig; a three-pronged electrical plug that can only be plugged in one way. Called "poka-yoke" by the Japanese.

Failure mode and effects analysis (FMEA) - A methodology for analyzing products for failure types in order to prevent customer dissatisfaction. Potential failure modes or types are developed by process and design teams. The effects on customer and process are estimated. Causes are defined and occurrence, detection capability, and severity are assessed. A risk priority is assigned and corrective action is instituted. An FMEA report format is used to facilitate this activity.

Families - A group of end items whose similarity of design and manufacture facilitates being planned in aggregate, whose sales performance is monitored together, and occasionally whose cost is aggregated at this level.

Feedback - The flow of information back into the control system so actual performance can be compared with planned performance.

File - An organized collection of records or the storage device in which these records are kept.

Final assembly - (1) The highest level of assembled product, as it is shipped to customers. (2) The name for the manufacturing department where the product is assembled. Synonym: erection department; blending department; pack out department.

Final assembly schedule (FAS) - Also referred to as "finishing schedule," because it may include other operations than simply the final operations. It may also not involve "assembly" but only final mixing, cutting, packaging, and so on. It is a schedule of end items to finish the product for specific customer orders in a "make-to-order" or "assemble-to-order" environment. It is prepared after receipt of a customer order as constrained by the availability of material and capacity, and it schedules the operations required to complete the product from the level where it is stocked (or master scheduled) to the end-item level. Synonym: blending; schedule; pack out schedule.

Firm planned order (FPO) - A planned order that can be frozen in quan-

tity and time. The computer is not allowed to automatically change it; this is the responsibility of the planner in charge of the item that is being planned. This technique can aid planners to respond to material, supplier, and capacity problems by firming selected planned orders. Additionally, firm planned orders are the normal method of stating the master production schedule.
Fishbone chart - See cause and effect diagram.
Fitness for use - Involves the quality of a product and/or the appropriateness of its design characteristics for its intended use by internal or external customers.
Fixed cost - An expenditure that does not vary with the production volume; for example: rent; property tax, salaries of certain personnel. See variable cost.
Fixed order quantity - A lot-sizing technique for inventory management that will always cause planned or actual orders to be generated for a predetermined fixed quantity or multiples thereof if net requirements for the period exceed the fixed order quantity. See economic order quantity; lot-for-lot; period order quantity.
Flow control - A term used to describe a specific production control system that is based primarily on setting production rates and feeding work into production to meet these planned rates, then following it through production to make sure that it is moving. Flow control has its most successful application in repetitive production. See order control.
Flow shop - A form of manufacturing organization in which machines and operators handle a standard, usually uninterrupted, material flow. The operators tend to perform the same operations for each production run. A flow shop is often referred to as a mass production shop, or is said to have a continuous manufacturing layout. The plant layout (arrangement of machines, benches, assembly lines, etc.) is designed to facilitate a product "flow." The process industries (chemicals, oil, paint, etc.) are extreme examples of flow shops. Each product, though variable in material specifications, uses the same flow pattern through the shop. Production is set at a given rate, and the products are generally manufactured in bulk.
Fluctuation inventory - Inventories that are carried as a cushion to protect against forecast error. See safety stock.
Focus forecasting - A system that allows the user to simulate the effectiveness of numerous forecasting techniques, thereby being able to select the most effective one.
Focused factory - A plant or production group set up as a separate entity

to produce a specific number of products and/or employ a limited number of processes.
Forecast - An estimate of future demand. A forecast can be determined by mathematical means using historical data; it can be created subjectively by using estimates from informal sources; or it can represent a combination of both techniques. See extrinsic forecast; intrinsic forecast.
Forecast consumption - The process of replacing the forecast with customer orders, or other types of actual demands, as they are received.
Forecast error - The difference between actual demand and forecast demand, stated as an absolute value or as a percentage.
Gantt chart - A control chart especially designed to show graphically the relationship between planned performance and actual performance, named after its originator, Henry L. Gantt. Used for machine loading, where one horizontal line is used to represent capacity and another to represent load against that capacity, or for following job progress where one horizontal line represents the production schedule and another parallel line represents the actual progress of the job against the schedule in time. Often used in project planning. Synonym: job progress chart.
Gross requirement - The total of independent and dependent demand for a component prior to the netting of on-hand inventory and scheduled receipts.
Group technology - An engineering and manufacturing philosophy that identifies the "sameness" of parts, equipment, or processes. It provides for rapid retrieval of existing designs and anticipates a cellular type production equipment layout.
Handling cost - The cost involved in handling inventory. In some cases, the handling cost incurred may depend on the size of the inventory.
Heuristic - A form of problem solving where the results or rules have been determined by experience or intuition instead of by optimization.
Idle time - Time when operators or machines are not producing product because of setup, maintenance, lack of material, tooling. Synonym: downtime.
Inbound stock point - A defined location next to the place of use on a production flow to which materials are brought as needed, and from which material is taken for immediate use. Used with a pull system of material control. See Just-in-Time.
Indented bill of material - A form of multilevel bill of material. It exhibits the highest-level parents closest to the left side margin, and all the components going into these parents are shown indented to the right of the

margin. All subsequent levels of components are indented farther to the right. If a component is used in more than one parent within a given product structure, it will appear more than once, under every sub-assembly in which it is used.

Independent demand - Demand for an item is considered independent when such demand is unrelated to the demand for other items. Demand for finished goods, parts required for destructive testing, and service parts requirements are some examples of independent demand. See dependent demand.

Independent demand inventory system - The policies, methods, and procedures used to manage inventory items that have independent demand. See independent demand; order point system.

Indirect cost - Cost not directly incurred by a particular job or operation. Certain utility costs, such as plant heating, are often indirect. An indirect cost is typically distributed to the product through the overhead rates. See direct cost.

Indirect labor - Work required to support production in general without being related to a specific product; for example, floor sweeping.

Indirect materials - Materials that become part of the final product but in such small quantities their cost is not applied directly to the product. Instead, their expense becomes a part of manufacturing supply or over-head costs.

Infinite loading - Showing the work behind work centers in the time periods required regardless of the capacity available to perform this work. The term infinite loading is considered to be obsolete today, although the specific computer programs used to do infinite loading can now be used to perform the technique called "capacity requirements planning." Infinite loading was a gross misnomer to start with, implying that a load could be put into a factory regardless of its availability to perform. The poor terminology obscured the fact that it is necessary to generate capacity requirements and compare these with available capacity before trying to adjust requirements to capacity. See capacity requirements planning; finite loading.

Internal setup time - Elements of a setup procedure performed while the process is not running. Ant: external setup time.

Interoperation time - The time between the completion of one operation and the start of the next. See move time.

Interplant demand - Items to be shipped to another plant or division within the corporation. Although it is not a customer order, it is usually

handled by the master production scheduling system in a similar manner. See demand management.
In-transit inventory - Material moving between two or more locations, usually separated geographically; for example, the shipment of finished goods from a plant to a distribution center.
Inventory - Items that are in a stocking location or work in process and that serve to decouple successive operations in the process of manufacturing a product and distributing it to the consumer. Inventories may consist of finished goods ready for sale; they may be parts or intermediate items; they may be work in process; or they may be raw materials.
Inventory buffer - See fluctuation inventory.
Inventory control - The activities and techniques of maintaining the stock of items at desired levels, whether they are raw materials, work in process, or finished products.
Inventory investment - The number of dollars that are tied up in all levels of inventory.
Inventory turnover - The number of times that an inventory "turns over," or cycles during the year. A frequently used method to compute inventory turnover is to divide the average inventory level into the annual cost of sales; for example, if average inventory were $3 million and cost of sales were $21 million, the inventory would be considered to "turn" seven times per year.
Inventory valuation - The value of the inventory at either its cost or its market value. Because inventory value can change with time, some recognition is taken of the age distribution of inventory. Therefore, the cost of value of inventory is usually computed on a first-in-first-out (FIFO), or a last-in-first-out (LIFO) basis, or a standard cost basis to establish the cost of goods sold.
Ishikawa diagram - See cause-and-effect diagram.
Issue - The physical movement of items from a stocking location. Often, also refers to the transaction reporting of this activity. See planned issue.
Item - Any unique manufactured or purchased part, material, intermediate, subassembly, or product.
Item number - A number that serves to uniquely identify an item. Synonym: part number; stock code.
Item record - The "master" record for an item. Typically it contains identifying and descriptive data, control values (lead times, lot sizes) and may contain data on inventory status, requirements, planned orders, and costs. Item records are linked together by bill of material records (or product

structure records), thus defining the bill of material.
Jidoka - Practice of stopping the production line when a defect occurs.
JIT See Just-in-Time.
Job order costing - A costing system in which costs are collected to specific jobs. Also called "job costing." This system can be used with either actual or standard costs in the manufacturing of distinguishable units or lots of products.
Job shop - Typically a make-to-order manufacturing plant. Products are made in intermittent sequences as defined by specific customer orders. Ant: flow shop. See make-to-order product.
Just-in-Time (JIT) - Having only the correct quality part in the right place at the right time. The implication is that each operation is so closely synchronized with the subsequent ones that the signal to perform work in any station is from the downstream station. In the broad sense, an approach to achieving excellence in a manufacturing company based on the continuing elimination of waste (waste being those things that do not add value to the product). See zero inventories.
Kanban - A method of signaling in Just-in-Time production that uses standard containers or lot sizes with a single card attached to each. It is a pull system in which work centers signal with a card that they wish to withdraw parts from feeding operations or suppliers. Kanban, in Japanese, loosely translated means "card," literally "billboard" or "sign." The term is often used synonymously for the specific scheduling system developed and used by Toyota Corporation in Japan.
Kit - The components of a parent that have been pulled from stock and readied for movement to a production area.
Lead-time - A span of time required to perform an activity. In a logistics context, the time between recognition of the need for an order and the receipt of goods. Individual components of lead-time can include: order preparation time, queue time, move or transportation time, receiving and inspection time. See manufacturing lead time; purchasing lead time.
Lead time offset - A technique used in MRP where a planned order receipt in one time period will require the release of that order in an earlier time period based on the lead time for the item.
Learning curve - A planning technique particularly useful in project-oriented industries where new products are phased in rather frequently. The basis for the learning curve calculation is the fact that workers will be able to produce the product more quickly after they get used to making it. For example, in a 90 percent learning curve, every time the quantity to

make doubles, the time to do the work drops to 90 percent of the previous time to do the work.
Level - Every part or assembly in a product structure is assigned a level code signifying the relative level in which that part or assembly is used within that product structure. Normally, the end items are assigned level "0" with the components/subassemblies going into it assigned level "1" and so on. MRP explosion process starts from level "0" and proceeds downward one level at a time.
Line balancing - The assignment, organizing, and equalizing of sequential tasks through workstations to minimize the number of workstations and idle time at all stations, to balance (match) the amount of work time at each station. Any assembly line process can be divided into elemental tasks, each with a specified time requirement per unit of product and a sequence relationship with the other tasks. Line balancing can also mean a technique for determining the product mix that can be run down an assembly line to provide a fairly consistent flow of work through that assembly line at the planned line rate.
Load leveling - Spreading orders out in time or so rescheduling operations that the amount of work to be done in sequential time periods tends to be distributed evenly and is achievable. See finite loading.
Logistics - In an industrial context, this term refers to the art and science of obtaining and distributing material and product. In a military sense, its meaning can also include the movement of personnel and spare parts.
Lot - A quantity produced together and sharing the same production costs and resultant specifications.
Lot-for-lot - A lot-sizing technique that generates planned orders in quantities equal to the net requirements in each period. Synonym: discrete order quantity.
Lot number - A unique identification assigned to a homogenous quantity of material. Synonym: batch number; mix number.
Lot number control - Assignment of unique numbers to each instance of receipt and carrying forth that number into subsequent manufacturing processes so that, in review of an end item, each lot consumed from raw materials through end item can be identified as having been used for the manufacture of this specific end item lot.
Lot size - The amount of a particular item that is ordered from the plant or a supplier. Synonym: order quantity.
Lot traceability - The ability to identify the lot or batch numbers of consumption and/or composition for manufactured, purchased, and shipped

items. This is a federal requirement in certain regulated industries.
Low-level code - Identifies the lowest level in any bill of material at which a particular component may appear. Net requirements for a given component are not calculated until all the gross requirements have been calculated down to that level. Low-level codes are normally calculated and maintained automatically by the computer software. See level.
Lumpy demand - A demand pattern with large fluctuations from one time period to another. Synonym: discontinuous demand.
Maintenance repair and operating supplies (MRO) - Items used in support of general operations and maintenance, such as maintenance supplies, spare parts, consumables used in the manufacturing process.
Major setup - The equipment setup and related activities required to manufacture a group of items in sequence, exclusive of the setup required for each item in the group. Ant: minor setup.
Make-or-buy decision - The act of deciding whether to produce an item in-house or buy it from an outside supplier.
Make-to-order product - A product that is finished after receipt of a customer order. Frequently long lead-time components are planned prior to the order arriving to reduce the delivery time to the customer. Where options or other subassemblies are stocked prior to customer orders arriving, the term assemble-to-order is frequently used. See job shop.
Make-to-stock product - A product shipped from finished goods, "off the shelf," and therefore is finished prior to a customer order arriving.
Manufacturing calendar - A calendar, used in inventory and production planning functions, that consecutively numbers only the working days so the component and work order scheduling may be done based on the actual number of work days available. Synonym: M-day calendar.
Manufacturing lead-time - The total time required to manufacture an item, exclusive of purchasing lead-time. Included here are order preparation time, queue time, setup time, run time, move time, inspection, and put-away time.
Manufacturing order - A document, group of documents, or schedule identity conveying authority for the manufacture of specified parts or products in specified quantities.
Manufacturing process - The series of activities performed on a material to convert it from the raw or semi-finished state to a state of further completion and a greater value.
Manufacturing resource planning (MRP II) - A method for the effective planning of all resources of a manufacturing company. Ideally, it

addresses operational planning in units, financial planning in dollars, and has a simulation capability to answer "what if" questions. It is made up of a variety of functions, each linked together: business planning, sales, and operations (production planning), master production scheduling, material requirements planning, capacity requirements planning, and the execution support systems for capacity and material. Output from these systems would be integrated with financial reports, such as the business plan, purchase commitment report, shipping budget, inventory projection in dollars, and so on. Manufacturing resource planning is a direct outgrowth and extension of closed-loop MRP. See closed-loop MRP; material requirements planning.
Manufacturing strategy - A collective pattern of decisions that act on the formulation and deployment of manufacturing resources. To be most effective, the manufacturing strategy should act in support of the overall strategic direction of the business unit and provide competitive advantage where called for.
Master production schedule (MPS) - The anticipated build schedule for those items assigned to the master scheduler. The master scheduler maintains this schedule and, in turn, it becomes a set of planning numbers that "drives" material requirements planning. It represents what the company plans to produce expressed in specific configurations, quantities, and dates. The master production schedule is not a sales forecast, which represents a statement of demand. The master production schedule must take into account the forecast, the production plan, and other important considerations, such as backlog, availability of material, avail-ability of capacity, management policy, and goals. Synonym: master schedule. See closed-loop MRP.
Master scheduler - The job title of the person who manages the master production schedule. This person should be the best scheduler available, because the consequences of the planning done here have a great impact on material and capacity planning. Ideally, the person would have substantial product and plant knowledge.
Material planner - The person normally responsible for managing the inventory levels, schedules, and availability of selected items, either manufactured or purchased. In an MRP system, the person responsible for reviewing and acting on order release, action, and exception messages from the system.
Material requirements planning (MRP) - A set of techniques that uses bills of material, inventory data, and the master production schedule to

calculate requirements for materials. It makes recommendations to release replenishment orders for material. Further, since it is time phased, it makes recommendations to reschedule open orders when due dates and need dates are not in phase. Originally seen as merely a better way to order inventory, today it is thought of as primarily a scheduling technique, (i.e., a method for establishing and maintaining valid due dates—priorities) on orders. See closed-loop MRP; manufacturing resource planning.

Materials management - The grouping of management functions supporting the complete cycle of material flow, from the purchase and internal control of production materials to the planning and control of work in process to the warehousing, shipping, and distribution of the finished product.

Material usage variance - The difference between the planned or standard requirements for materials to produce a given item and the actual quantity used for this particular instance of manufacture.

Material yield - The ratio of usable material from a given quantity. Synonym: potency.

Matrix bill of material - A chart made up from the bills of material for a number of products in the same or similar families. It is arranged in a matrix with components in columns and parents in rows (or vice versa) so requirements for common components can be summarized conveniently.

Mean - The arithmetic average of a group of values.

Mean absolute deviation (MAD) - The average of the absolute values of the deviations of some observed value from some expected value. MAD can be calculated based on observations and the arithmetic mean of those observations. An alternative is to calculate absolute deviations of actual sales data minus forecast data. These data can be averaged in the usual arithmetic way or with exponential smoothing.

Min-max system - A type of order point replenishment system where the "min" is the order point and the "max" is the "order-up-to" inventory level. The order quantity is variable and is the result of the "max" minus on-hand and on-order inventory. An order is recommended when the on-hand and on-order inventory is at or below the "min."

Mixed-model production - Making several different parts or products in varying lot sizes so a factory is making close to the same mix of products that will be sold that day. The mixed-model schedule governs the making and the delivery of component parts, including outside suppliers. The goal is to build every model, every day, according to demand.

Modular bill (of material) - A type of planning bill that is arranged in product modules or options. Often used in companies where the product has many optional features, (e.g., automobiles). See planning bill; common parts bill; super bill.

Move card - In a Just-in-Time context, refers to a card or other signal indicating that a specific number of units of a particular item are to be taken from a source (usually outbound stock point) and taken to a point of use (usually inbound stock point). Synonym: move signal. See kanban; production card.

Move order - The authorization to move a particular item from one location to another.

Move ticket - A document used in dispatching to authorize and/or record movement of a job from one work center to another. It may also be used to report other information, such as the active quantity or the material storage location.

MPS - See master production schedule.

MRP - See material requirements planning.

MRP II - See manufacturing resource planning.

Multilevel bill of material - A display of all the components directly or indirectly used in a parent, together with the quantity required of every component. If a component is a subassembly, blend, intermediate, and the like, all of its components will also be exhibited and all of their components, down to purchased parts and materials.

Multilevel where used - A display for a component listing all the parents in which that component is directly used and the next higher level parents into which each of those parents is used, until ultimately all top-level (level 0) parents are listed.

Need date - The date when an item is required for its intended use. In an MRP system, this date is calculated by a bill of material explosion of a schedule and the netting of available inventory against that requirement. See due date.

Net requirements - In MRP, the net requirements for a part or an assembly are derived as a result of applying gross requirements and allocations against inventory on hand, scheduled receipts, and safety stock. Net requirements, lot sized and offset for lead-time, become planned orders.

Netting - The process of calculating net requirements.

Normal distribution - A particular statistical distribution where most of the observations fall fairly close to one mean, and a deviation from the mean is as likely to be plus as it is likely to be minus. When graphed, the

normal distribution takes the form of a bell-shaped curve.
Obsolescence - Loss of product value resulting from a model or style change or technological development. See deterioration.
On-hand balance - The quantity shown in the inventory records as being physically in stock. See available inventory.
On-order - The quantity of stock on-order represented by the total of all out-standing replenishment orders. The on-order balance increases when a new order is released and it decreases when material is received against an order, or when an order is cancelled. See on-hand balance; open order.
Open order - (1) A released manufacturing order or purchase order. Synonym: scheduled receipt. (2) An unfilled customer order.
Operation duration - The total time that elapses between the start of setup of an operation and the completion of the operation.
Operation priority - The scheduled due date and/or start date of a specific operation for a specific job, usually as determined by the back scheduling process. See back scheduling; dispatching; order priority.
Operation sequencing - A simulation technique for short-term planning of actual jobs to be run in each work center based on capacity, priority, existing manpower, and machine availability.
Operation sequence - The sequential steps for an item to follow in its flow through the plant. For instance, operation 1: cut bar stock; operation 2: grind bar stock; operation 3: shape; operation 4: polish; operation 5: inspect and send to stock. This information is normally maintained in the routing file.
Operating start date - The date when an operation should be started for its order due date to be met. It can be calculated based on scheduled quantities and lead times (queue, setup, run, move) or based on the work remaining and the time remaining to complete the job.
Order entry - The process of accepting and translating what a customer wants into terms used by the manufacturer or distributor. This can be as simple as creating shipping documents for a finished good product line, to a more complicated series of activities including engineering effort for make-to-order products.
Ordering cost - Used in calculating economic order quantities, and it refers to the costs that increase as the number of orders placed increases. Includes costs related to the clerical work of preparing, releasing, following, and receiving orders, the physical handling of goods, inspections, and setup costs, as applicable. Synonym: acquisition cost. Ant: carrying costs.
Order multiples - An order quantity modifier applied after the lot size has

been calculated that increments the order quantity to a predetermined multiple.
Order point - A set inventory level where, if the total stock on-hand plus on-order falls to or below that point, action is taken to replenish the stock. The order point is normally calculated as historical or forecasted usage during the replenishment lead-time plus safety stock. Synonym: reorder point; trigger level. See time-phased order point.
Order point system - The method whereby replenishment orders are triggered (launched) at a calculated inventory level. See order point; time-phased order point; two bi; min-max.
Order promising - The process of making a delivery commitment (i.e., answering the question, "When can you ship?"). For make-to-order products, this usually involves a check of uncommitted material and availability of capacity. Synonym: order dating; customer order promising. See available-to-promise.
Output - (1) Work being completed by a production facility. (2) The result of a computer program.
Overhead - Costs incurred in the operation of a business that cannot be directly related to the individual products or services produced. These costs, such as light, heat, supervision, and maintenance, are grouped in several pools (department overhead, factory overhead, general over-head) and distributed to units of product, or service, by some standard method, such as direct labor hours, direct labor dollars, direct materials dollars. See Burden.
Paperless purchasing - A purchasing operation that does not employ purchase requisitions or hard-copy purchase orders. In actual practice, a small amount of "paperwork" usually remains, normally in the form of the vendor schedule. See Just-in-Time; supplier scheduling.
Pareto's law - A concept developed by Vilfredo Pareto, an Italian economist, which states that a small percentage of a group accounts for the largest fraction of the impact, value, and so on; for example, 20 percent of the inventory items may comprise 80 percent of the inventory value. Synonym: 80/20 rule. See ABC classification.
Part - Normally refers to a material item used as a component and is not an assembly, subassembly blend, intermediate, and so on. See component.
Part number - See item number.
Past due - An order that has not been completed on the date scheduled. Synonym: delinquent.
Performance standard - A criterion or benchmark against which actual

performance is compared.

Periodic inventory - A physical inventory taken at some recurring interval (e.g., monthly, quarterly, or annual physical inventory).

Perpetual inventory - An inventory recordkeeping system where each transaction in and out is recorded and a new balance is computed.

Perpetual inventory record - A computer record or manual document on which each inventory transaction is posted so an accurate record of the inventory is maintained. See on-hand balance.

Phantom bill of material - A bill of material coding and structuring technique used primarily for transient (non-stocked) subassemblies. For the transient item, lead-time is set to zero and the order quantity to lot-for-slot. This permits MRP logic to drive requirements straight through the phantom item to its components, but usually retains its ability to net against any occasional inventories of the item. This technique also facilitates the use of common bills of material for engineering and manufacturing. Synonym: transient bill of material; blow-though.

Physical inventory - (1) The actual inventory itself. (2) The determination of inventory quantity by actual count. Physical inventories can be taken on a continuous, periodic, or annual basis. See cycle counting.

Picking - The process of withdrawing from stock the components to make the products, or the finished goods to be shipped to a customer.

Planned issue - A disbursement of an item predicted by MRP through the creation of a gross requirement or allocation.

Planned load - The standard hours of work required by MRP recommended (planned) production orders. See planned order.

Planned order - A suggested order quantity, release date, and due date created by MRP processing, when it encounters net requirements. Planned orders are created by the computer, exist only within the computer, and may be changed or deleted by the computer during subsequent MRP processing if conditions change. Planned orders at one level will be exploded into gross requirements for components at the next lower level. Planned orders, along with released orders, also served as input to capacity requirements planning, to show the total capacity requirements in future time periods. See firm planned order; open order; scheduled receipt.

Planned receipt - A receipt against an open purchase order or open production order that has not yet been received.

Planning bill (of material) - An artificial grouping of items and/or events, in bill of material format, used to facilitate master scheduling and/or material planning. See common parts bill; modular bill; super bill.

Planning horizon - The span of time from the current to some future point for which plans are generated.

Post-deduct - See backflush

Poka-yoke - Mistake-proofing techniques, such as manufacturing or setup activity designed in a way to prevent an error from resulting in a product defect. For example, in an assembly operation, if each correct part is not used, a sensing device detects a part was unused and shuts down the operation, thereby preventing the assembler from moving the incomplete part on to the next station or beginning another one.

Preventive maintenance - A routine pattern of tests, checks, analysis, or replacements based on history, run time, cycles or operating characteristics. The purpose of these actions is to prevent unplanned shutdown. A good preventive maintenance program will extend equipment life, increase throughput, and increase productivity. Sometimes called Total Productive Maintenance (TPM).

Primary work center - The work center wherein an operation on a manufactured part is normally scheduled to be performed. Antonym: alternate work center.

Priority - In a general sense, refers to the relative importance of jobs or activities (i.e., the sequence in time on which jobs should be worked). See capacity; scheduling.

Priority control - The process of communicating start and completion dates to manufacturing departments to execute a plan. The dispatch list is the tool normally used to provide these dates based on the current plan and status of all open orders.

Priority planning - The function of determining what material is needed and when. Master production scheduling and material requirements planning are the elements used for the planning and re-planning process to maintain proper due dates on required materials.

Process costing - A cost accounting system in which the costs are collected by time and averaged over all the units produced during the period.

Process flow production - A production approach with minimal interruptions in actual processing in any one production run or between production runs of similar products. Queue time is virtually eliminated by integrating the moving of the product into the actual operation of the resource performing the work.

Process manufacturing - Production that adds value by mixing, separating, forming, and/or chemical reactions. It may be done in either batch or continuous mode.

Process sheet - Detailed manufacturing instructions issued to the plant. The instructions may include speeds, feed rates, temperatures, tools, fixtures, machines, inspections, and sketches of setups and semi-finished dimensions. See routing.

Process time - The time during which the material is being worked, whether it is a machining operation or a hand assembly. Synonym: residence time; cycle time.

Procurement lead time - The time required by the buyer to select a supplier and to place and obtain a commitment for specific quantities of material at specified times. The time between the receipt of a requirement to buy and the time the purchase is completed. See purchasing lead time.

Product family - A group of products with similar characteristics, often used in sales and operations (production) planning.

Product group forecast - A forecast for a number of similar products.

Production card - In a Just-in-Time context, it refers to a card or other signal for indicating that items should be made for use or to replace some items removed from pipeline stock. See kanban; move card.

Production control - The function of directing or regulating the movement of goods through the entire manufacturing cycle from the requisitioning of raw material to the delivery of the finished products. See inventory control.

Production cycle - The lead-time to produce a product. See cycle.

Production forecast - A predicted level of customer demand for an option, feature, and so on, of an assemble-to-order product (or finish-to-order product). It is calculated by netting customer backlog against an overall family or product line master production schedule and then factoring this product "available-to-promise" by the option percentage in a planning bill of material.

Production line - A series of equipment or resources dedicated to the manufacture of a specific number of products or families.

Production plan - The agreed-on plan that comes from the sales and operation (production) planning function, specifically the overall level or rate of manufacturing output to be produced. Usually stated as a monthly rate for each product family (group of products, items, options, features, and so on). Various units of measure can be used to express the plan: units, tonnage, standard hours, number of workers. The production plan is management's authorization for the master scheduler to convert it into a more detailed plan; that is, the master production schedule. See sales and operations planning.

Production schedule - A plan that authorizes the factory to manufacture a certain quantity of a specific item. Usually initiated by the production.

Planning department - See work order; manufacturing order.

Productivity - Refers to a relative measure of output per labor and/or machine input. An overall measure of production effectiveness is composed of two factors: efficiency (how well a resource is performing) and utilization (how intensively a resource is being used). It is calculated (1) as the product of the efficiency and utilization factors or (2) as the ratio of the output achieved as measured in standard hours to the total clock time scheduled for production for a given time period.

Productivity = Efficiency x Utilization

or

Productivity = Standard hours of output + Clock time scheduled

Product layout - See continuous production.

Product load profile - A listing of the required capacity and key resources required to manufacture one unit of a selected item or family. Often used to predict the impact of the item scheduled on the overall schedule and load of the key resources. Rough cut capacity planning uses these pro-files to calculate the approximate capacity requirements of the master production schedule and/or the production plan. Synonym: bill of labor; bill of resources; resource profile.

Product mix - The proportion of individual products that make up the total production and/or sales volume. Changes in the product mix can mean drastic changes in the manufacturing requirements for certain types of labor and material.

Product structure - The way components go into a product during its manufacture. A typical product structure or multilevel bill of material would show raw material converted into fabricated components, components put together to make subassemblies, subassemblies going into assemblies, and so forth.

Projected available balance - In MRP, the inventory balance projected into the future. It is the running sum of on-hand inventory minus requirements plus scheduled receipts and planned orders. See projected on hand.

Projected on hand - Same as projected available balance, except excludes planned order.

Pull (system) - (1) In production, it refers to the production of items only as demanded for use, or to replace those taken for use. (2) In a material control context, it refers to the withdrawal of inventory as demanded by the using operations. Material is not issued until a signal comes from the user. (3) In distribution, it refers to a system for replenishing field warehouse inventories wherein replenishment decisions are made at the field warehouse itself, not at the central warehouse or plant. Ant: push system.

Purchase part - An item purchased from a supplier.

Purchase requisition - A document conveyed to the purchasing department to request the purchase of materials in specified quantities within a specified time.

Purchasing capacity - The act of buying capacity or machine time from a supplier. This allows a company to use and schedule the capacity of the machine or a part of the capacity of the machine as if it were in its own plant. This also shortens lead-time by eliminating queue time at the supplier.

Purchasing lead-time - The total lead-time required to obtain a purchased item. Included here are order preparation and release time, supplier lead-time, transportation time, receiving, inspections, and put-away time.

Push (system) - (1) In production, it refers to the production of items at times required by a given schedule planned in advance. (2) In material control, it refers to the issuing of material according to a given schedule and/or issued to a job order at its start time. (3) In distribution, it refers to a system for replenishing field warehouse inventories wherein replenishment decision making is centralized, usually at the manufacturing site or central supply facility. Ant: pull system.

Quality - Conformance to requirements.

Quality at the source - A producer's responsibility to provide 100 percent acceptable quality material to the consumer of the material. The objective is to reduce or eliminate shipping/receiving quality inspections and line stoppages as a result of supplier defects.

Quality circle - A small group of people who normally work as a unit and meet frequently for the purpose of uncovering and solving problems concerning the quality of items produced, process capability or process control. Synonym: quality control circle; self-directed work group.

Quality control - The function of verifying conformance to requirements.

Quantity discount - An allowance determined by the quantity or value of a purchase.

Queue - A waiting line. In manufacturing, the jobs at a given work center waiting to be processed. As queues increase, so do average queue time and work-in-process inventory.

Rang - The statistical term referring to the spread in a series of observa-

tions. For example, the anticipated demand for a particular product might vary from a low of 10 to a high of 500 per week. The range would, therefore, be 500 – 10 or 490.
Rated capacity - Capacity calculated from such data as utilization and efficiency, hours planned to be worked, and so on. Synonym: theoretical capacity. Ant: demonstrated capacity.
Raw in process (RIP) - Inventory kept on the shop floor but not issued to any work order or product. Free stock. Usually a segregating of stockroom inventory from floor inventory accomplished by transferring location from stockroom to shop location. Backflushing or postdeduct relieves the RIP location.
Raw material - Purchased items or extracted materials that will be converted by the manufacturing process into components and/or products.
Receiving - This function includes the physical receipt of material; the inspection of the shipment for conformance with the purchase order (quantity and damage); identification and delivery to destination; and preparing receiving reports.
Record accuracy - The conformity of recorded values in a bookkeeping system to the actual values. For example, the on hand balance of an item maintained in a computer record relative to the actual on hand balance of the items in the stockroom.
Regeneration MRP - An MRP processing approach where the master production schedule is totally re-exploded down through all bills of material, to maintain valid priorities. New requirements and planned orders are completely "regenerated" at that time. Ant: net change MRP; requirements alteration.
Released order - See open order. See reorder point See order point.
Reorder quantity - (1) In an order point system of inventory planning, the fixed quantity which should be ordered each time the available stock (on hand plus on order) falls below the order point. (2) In a variable reorder quantity system, the amount ordered from time period to time period will vary. Synonym: replenishment order quantity. See economic order quantity; lot size.
Repetitive manufacturing - Production of discrete units, planned and executed to a schedule, usually at relatively high speeds and volumes. Material tends to move in a continuous flow during production, but different items may be produced sequentially within that flow. See Just-In-Time.
Replenishment lead-time - The total time that elapses from the moment it

is determined that a product is to be reordered until the product is back on the shelf available for use.
Replenishment period - The time between successive replenishment orders (i.e., replenishment interval). See replenishment lead-time.
Requirements explosion - The process of calculating the demand for the components of a parent item by multiplying the parent item requirements by the component usage quantity specified in the bill of material. See dependent demand; gross requirements; material requirements planning.
Resource - Anything required for production of product whose lack of availability would cause failure to meet the plan.
Return on investment - A financial measure of the relative return from an investment, usually expressed as a percentage or earnings produced by an asset to the amount invested in the asset.
Review period - The time between successive evaluations of inventory status to determine whether to reorder. See lead-time.
Rough cut capacity planning - The process of converting the production plan and/or the master production schedule into capacity needs for key resources; manpower, machinery, warehouse space, suppliers' capabilities, and, in some cases, money. Product load profiles are often used to accomplish this. Synonym: resource requirements planning. See capacity requirements planning.
Routing - A set of information detailing the method of manufacture of a particular item. It includes the operations to be performed, their sequence, the various work centers to be involved, and the standards for setup and run. In some companies, the routing also includes information on tooling, operator skill levels, inspection operations, testing requirements, and the like.
Run time - The planned standard time to produce one or multiple units of an item in an operation. The actual time taken to produce one piece may vary from the standard, but the latter is used for loading purposes and is adjusted to actual by dividing by the appropriate work center efficiency factor.
Safety lead time - An element of time added to normal lead time for the purpose of completing an order in advance of its real need date. When used, the MRP system, in offsetting for lead-time, will plan both order release and order completion for earlier dates than it would otherwise. See safety stock.
Safety stock - (1) In general, a quantity of stock planned to be in inventory to protect against fluctuations in demand and/or supply. (2) In the

context of master production scheduling, safety stock can refer to additional inventory and/or capacity planned as protection against forecast errors and/or short-term changes in the backlog. Sometimes referred to as "overplanning" or a "market hedge." Synonym: buffer stock. See hedge.

Scheduled receipt - Within MRP, open production orders and open purchase orders are considered as "scheduled receipts." On their due date, they will be added to the projected available balance during the netting process for the time period in question. Scheduled receipt dates and/or quantities are not normally altered automatically by the MRP system. Further, scheduled receipts are not exploded into requirements for components, because MRP logic assumes that all components for the manufacture of the item in question have been either allocated or issued to the shop floor. See planned order; firm planned order.

Scheduler - A general term that can refer to material planner, dispatcher, or a combined function.

Scheduling - The act of creating a schedule, such as a master production schedule, shop schedule, maintenance schedule, vendor schedule.

Scheduling rules - Basic rules that can be used consistently in a scheduling system. Scheduling rules usually specify the amount of calendar time to allow for a move and for queue, how load will be calculated, and so on.

Scrap - Material outside of specifications and of such characteristics that rework is impractical.

Scrap factor - A percentage factor in the product structure used to increase gross requirements to account for anticipated loss within the manufacture of a particular product. See shrinkage factor.

Service parts - Parts used for the repair and/or maintenance of an assembled product. Typically they are ordered and shipped at a date later than the shipment of the product itself.

Service parts demand - The need for a component to be sold by itself, as opposed to being used in production to make a higher-level product. Synonym: repair parts demand; spare parts.

Setup - The process of changing dies or other parts of a machine to product a new part or product. Synonym: changeover.

Setup cost - The costs associated with a setup. Synonym: changeover cost.

Setup time - The time required for a specific machine, line, or work center to convert from the production of one specific item to another, typically from the last good part until the next (new) good part. See external setup time; internal setup time; major setup; minor setup.

Shelf life - The amount of time an item may be held in inventory before it becomes unusable.

Shipping - Provides facilities for the outgoing shipment of parts, products, and components. It includes packaging, marking, weighing, and loading for shipment.

Shop calendar - A special type of calendar used to facilitate scheduling. It is usually expressed in consecutively numbered working days and excludes weekends, holidays, plant shutdowns. See M-day calendar.

Shop floor control - A system for utilizing data from the shop floor to maintain and communicate status information on shop orders (manufacturing orders) and work centers. The major sub-functions of shop floor control are: (1) assigning priority of each shop order; (2) maintaining work-in-process quantity information; (3) conveying shop order status information to the office; (4) providing actual output data for capacity control purposes; (5) providing quantity by location by shop order for work-in-process inventory and accounting purposes; and (6) providing measurement of efficiency, utilization, and productivity of manpower and machines. Synonym: production activity control. See closed-loop MRP.

Shrinkage - Reductions of actual quantities of items in stock, in process, in transit. The loss may be caused by scrap, theft, deterioration, evaporation, and so on.

Shrinkage factor - A percentage factor in the item master record that compensates for expected loss during the manufacturing cycle either by increasing the gross requirements or by reducing the expected completion quantity of planned and open orders. The shrinkage factor differs from the scrap factor in that the former affects all uses of the part and its components, the scrap factor relates to only one usage. See scrap factor.

Simulation - (1) The technique of utilizing representative or artificial data to reproduce in a model various conditions that are likely to occur in the actual performance of a system. Frequently used to test the behavior of a system under different operating policies. (2) Within MRP II, utilizing the operational data to perform "what-if" evaluations of alternative plans, to answer the question "can we do it?" If yes, the simulation can then be run in financial mode to help answer the question "do we really want to?"

Single-level backflush - A form of backflush which reduces inventory on only the next-level-down parts used in an assembly or subassembly. See backflush; superflush.

Single-level bill of material - A display of those components that are directly used in a parent item. It shows only the relationships one level down.

Single minutes exchange of die (SMED) - The concept of setup times of less than 10 minutes, developed by Shigeo Shingo in 1970 at Toyota.

SKU - Abbreviation for stock keeping unit.

SPC - Abbreviation for statistical process control.

Staging - Pulling of the material for an order from inventory before the material is required. This action is often taken to identify shortages but can lead to increased problems in availability and inventory accuracy.

Standard costs - The target costs of an operation, process, or product including labor, material, and overhead charges.

Standard deviation - A measure of dispersion of data or of a variable. The standard deviation is computed by finding the difference between the average and actual observations, squaring each difference, summing the squared difference, finding the average squared difference (called the "variance") and taking the square root of the variance.

Standard error - Applied to statistics, such as the mean, to provide a distribution within which samples of the statistics are expected to fall. See: standard deviation.

Standard house - See standard time.

Standard time - The length of time that should be required to (a) set up a given machine or operation and (b) run one part/assembly/batch/end product through that operation. This time is used in determining machine requirements and labor requirements. Also, frequently used as a basis for incentive payrolls and cost accounting.

Start date - The date that an order or schedule should be released into the plant based on some form of scheduling rules. The start date should be early enough to allow time to complete the work, but not so early to overload the shop. See scheduling rules.

Statistical process control (SPC) - A quality control methodology that focuses on continuous monitoring during the production process itself, rather than postproduction inspection of the items produced. The intent is to not produce any defective items, by stopping the process before it drifts out of control.

Stock - (1) Items in inventory. (2) Stored products or service parts ready for sale as distinguished from stores that are usually components or raw materials.

Stockkeeping unit (SKU) - An item at a particular geographic location. For example, one product stock at six different distribution centers would represent six SKUs, plus perhaps another for the plant at which it was

manufactured.
Stockless production - See Just-in-Time.
Stock out - The lack of materials or components needed. See backorder.
Stock out costs - The lost sale and/or backorder cost incurred as a result of a stock out. See stock out.
Storage costs - A subset of inventory carrying costs, including the cost of warehouse utilities, material handling personnel, equipment maintenance, building maintenance, and security personnel. See carrying cost.
Subassembly - An assembly used at a higher level to make up another assembly. Synonym: intermediate. See component.
Suboptimization - A problem solution that is best from a narrow point of view but not from a higher or overall company point of view. For example, a department manager who would not work his department overtime to minimize his department's costs may be doing so at the expense of overall company profitability.
Summarized bill of material - A form of multilevel bill of material, which lists all the parts and their quantities required in a given product structure. Unlike the indented bill of material, it does not list the levels of manufacture and lists a component only once for the total quantity used.
Super bill (of material) - A type of planning bill, located at the top level in the structure, that ties together various modular bills (and possibly a common parts bill) to define an entire product or product family. The "quantity per" relationship of super bill to modules represents the fore-casted percentage of demand of each module. The master scheduled quantities of the super bill explode to create requirements for the modules that also are master scheduled. See planning bill; modular bill; common parts bill.
Superflush - A technique to relieve inventory of all components down to the lowest level using the complete bill of material, based on the count of finished units produced and/or transferred to finished goods inventory. See backflush; single-level backflush.
Supplier - A company or individual that supplies goods or services.
Supplier lead-time - The time that normally elapses between the time an order is received by the supplier and his shipment of the material.
Supplier measurement - The act of measuring the supplier's performance to the contract. Measurements usually cover delivery, quality, and price.
Supplier scheduling - A purchasing approach that provides suppliers with schedules, rather than individual hard-copy purchase orders. Normally, a supplier scheduling system will include a business agreement (contract)

for each supplier, a weekly (or more frequent) schedule for each supplier extending for some time into the future, and individuals called "supplier schedulers." Also required is a formal priority planning system that works very well, because it is essential in this arrangement to routinely provide the supplier with valid due dates. See Just-in-Time; paperless purchasing.
Synchronized production - A term sometimes used to mean repetitive Just-in-Time production.
Target inventory level - The equivalent of the "maximum" in a min-max system. The target inventory is equal to the order point plus the order quantity. It is often called an "order up to" inventory level and is used in a periodic review system. May also be the desired or planned inventory level in strategic business planning. See min-max system.
Teardown time - The time taken to remove a setup from a machine or facility. Teardown is an element of manufacturing lead time but often allowed for in setup or run time, rather than separately.
Throughput - The total volume of production, results, or actions through a facility or department, machine center, work cell, plant, or network of plants.
Time bucket - The time into which data is summarized. A weekly time bucket would contain all of the relevant data for an entire week. Weekly time buckets are considered to be the most reasonable term to permit effective MRP. See bucketless system.
Time fence - A policy or guideline established to manage where in time various updates or changes to operating plans or schedules take place. For example, changes to the master production schedule can be accomplished easily beyond the cumulative lead time to plan and build any product, whereas changes inside the cumulative lead time becomes increasingly more difficult to a point where changes should be resisted. Time fences can be used to define these points.
Time-phased order point (TPOP) - An order point technique MRP (or DRP) for independent demand items, where gross requirements come from a forecast, not via explosion generated from a dependent position in a bill of material. It is the basic logic structure of MRP calculations. It starts with onhand inventories, subtracts demand, adds incoming orders, and projects a new onhand balance. This technique can be used to plan distribution center inventories as well as planning for service (repair) parts or supplies. See distribution requirements planning (DRP).
Time phasing - The technique of expressing future sequential demand, supply, and inventories by time period. Time phasing is one of the key

elements of material requirements planning.

Time series - A set of data that is distributed over time, such as demand data in monthly time period occurrences.

Time standard - The predetermined times allowed for the performance of a specific job. The standard will often consist of two parts; that for machine or operation setup and that for actual work or running time. The standard can be developed through (1) observation of the actual work (time study), (2) summation of standard micromotion times (synthetic time standards, or (3) approximation from the analysis of historical job time.

Total productive maintenance - Preventive maintenance plus continuing efforts to adapt, modify, and refine equipment to increase flexibility, reduce material handling, and promote continuous flows. It is operator-oriented maintenance with the involvement of all qualified employees in all maintenance activities.

Total quality management (TQM) - An approach encompassing all phases of an organization, from marketing to delivery, that attempts to insure quality in all things, to ensure that no defective data, processes, or parts are produced in any department. The basic elements include: statistical quality control, process control, quality at the source, line stop, group problem solving, employee involvement, customer satisfaction, team building, and continuous improvement.

TPOP - Abbreviation for time-phased order point.

TQC - Abbreviation for total quality control. See total quality management.

Transit time - A standard allowance that is assumed on any given order for the physical movement of items from one operation to the next.

Transportation inventory - Inventory that is in transit between locations. See pipeline stock.

Turnover - (1) See inventory turnover. (2) In the United Kingdom and certain other countries, it refers to annual sales volume.

Two-bin system - A type of order point system in which inventory is carried in two bins. A replenishment quantity is ordered when the first bin is empty. When the material is received, the second bin is refilled and the excess is put into the working bin. This term is also used loosely to describe any order point system even when physical "bins" do not exist. Sometimes used in Just-In-Time manufacturing for small quantifies. See order point system.

U-lines - Production lines shaped like the letter "U." The shape allows workers to easily perform several different and interchangeable tasks without much walking. The number of workstations in a U-line are usually determined by line balancing and the process requirements. U-lines promote communication through cross training and close proximity. See cellular manufacturing; group technology.

Variable cost - An operating cost that varies directly with production volume; for example, materials consumed, direct labor, sales commissions. Ant: fixed cost.

Variance - (1) The difference between the expected (budgeted or planned) and the actual. (2) In statistics, the variance is a measure of dispersion of data.

Waste - A byproduct of a process or task with unique characteristics requiring special management control. Waste production can usually be planned and somewhat controlled. Scrap is typically not planned and may result from the same production run as waste. In total quality management, waste is any activity, materials, or capacity performed in any company activity that does not add value to the product or service.

Where-used - A listing of every parent item of any given component, and the respective quantity required, from a bill of material file.

WIP - See work in process.

Work center - A specific production facility, consisting of one or more people and/or machines, which can be considered as one unit for purposes of capacity requirements planning and detailed scheduling. See cost center.

Work in process (WIP) - Product or inventory in various stages of completion throughout the plant including raw material that has been released for initial processing, up to completely processed material awaiting final inspection and acceptance as finished product. Many accounting systems also include the value of semi-finished stock and components in this category. In Just-In-Time systems, work in process is not used because there are no work orders. Inventory is still in the raw material stock listings until it is backflushed and consumed into the finished product. See backflush; post-deduct. Synonym: in-process inventory.

Work order (WO) - The authorization order to commit resources to produce or fabricate a product or part. Frequently the term work order is used to designate orders to the machine shop for tool manufacture or maintenance. See manufacturing order.

Work station - The assigned location where a worker performs his or her job; it could be a machine or a work bench. See work center.

Zero inventories - A philosophy of manufacturing based on planned elimination of all waste and consistent improvement of productivity. It encompasses the successful execution of all manufacturing activities required to produce a final product, from design engineering to delivery and including all states of conversion from raw material onward. The primary elements of zero inventories are to have only the required inventory when needed; to improve quality to zero defects; to reduce lead times by reducing setup times, queue lengths, and lot sizes; and to incrementally revise the operations themselves to accomplish these things at minimum cost. In the broad sense it applies to all forms of manufacturing, job shop, and process, as well as repetitive. See Just-In-Time; stockless production.

Appendix B: References

The Just-In-Time Self-Test: Success through Assessment and Implementation. Fisher, Dennis. Irwin Professional Publishing, Chicago, 1995.

The Goal" by Eliyahu M. Goldrat, Jeff Cox. North River Press. 2004.

Kaizen: The Key to Japan's Competitive Success. Imai, Masaaki. Random House, New York, 1986.

Gemba Kaizen: A Commonsense, Low-Cost Approach to Management. Imai, Masaaki. McGraw-Hill, New York, 1997.